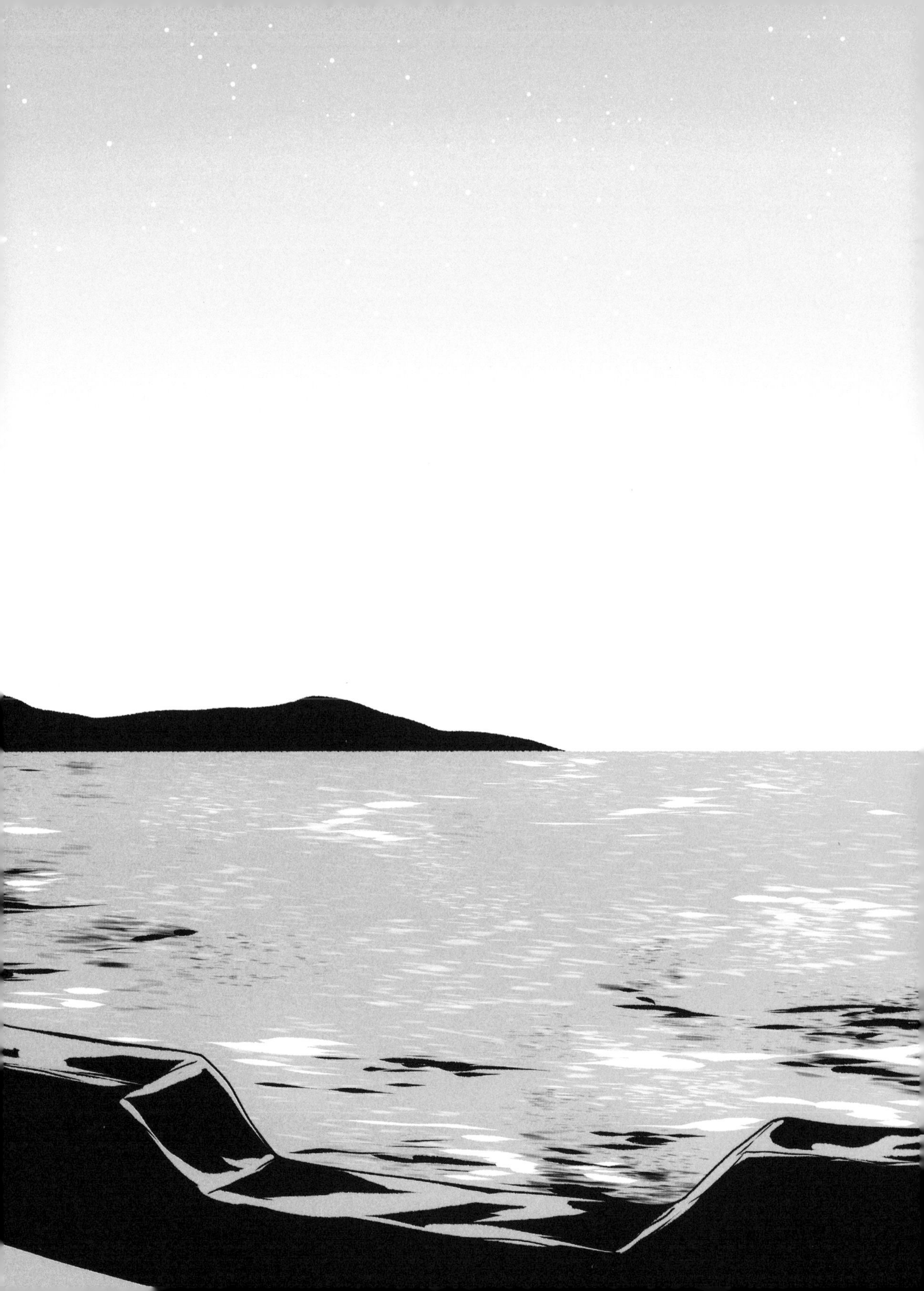

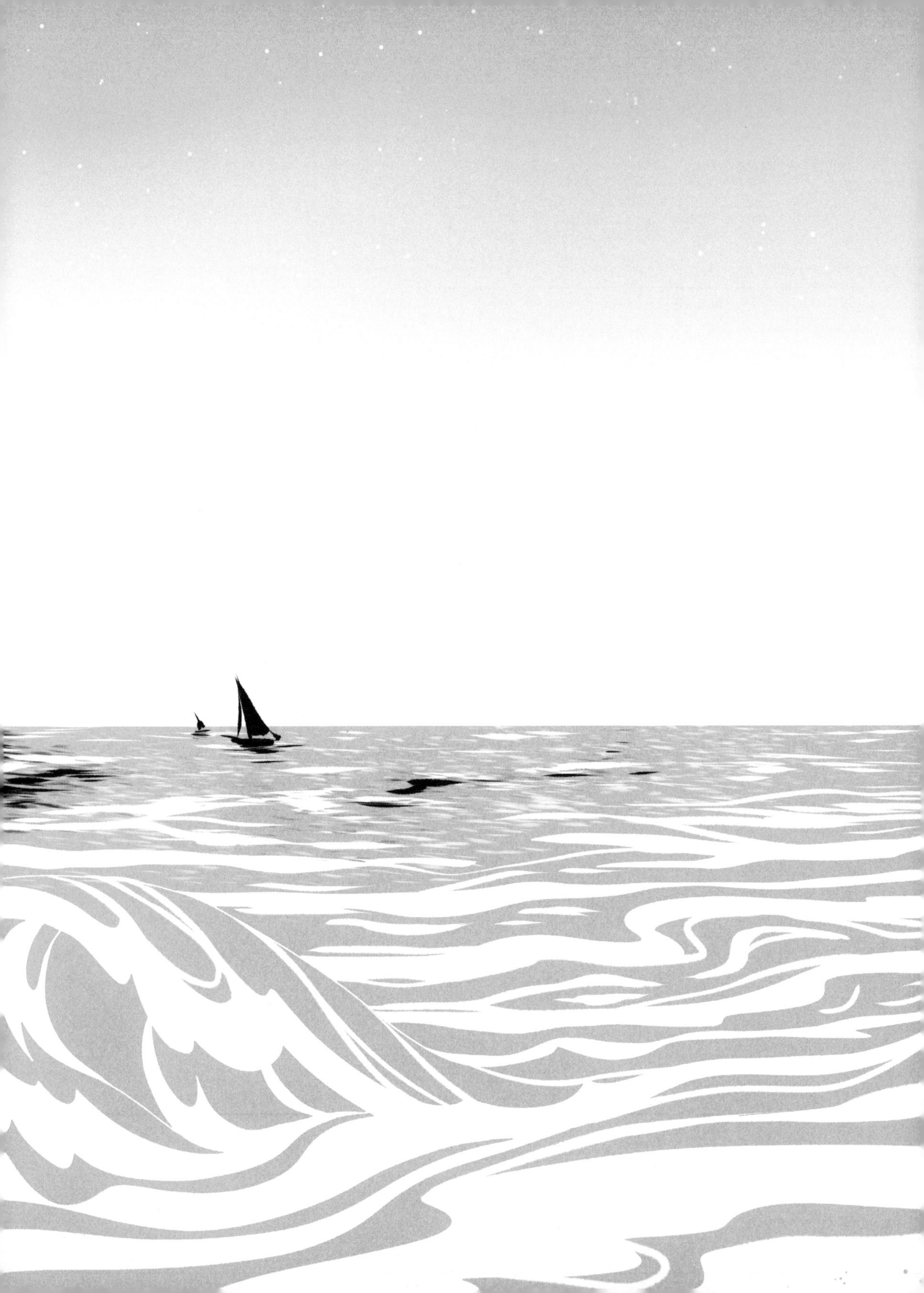

LIBERATED

THE RADICAL ART AND LIFE OF CLAUDE CAHUN

Kaz Rowe

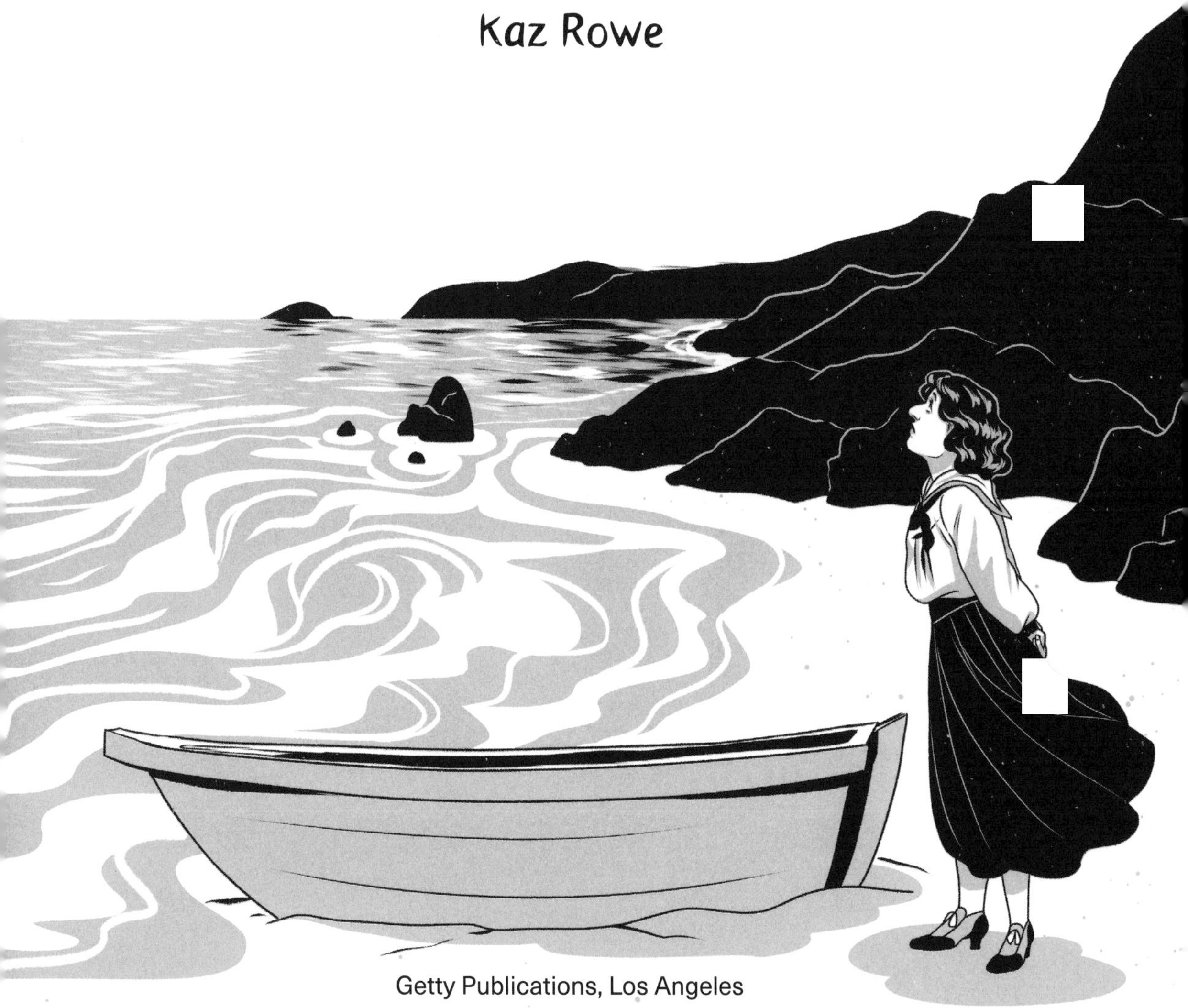

Getty Publications, Los Angeles

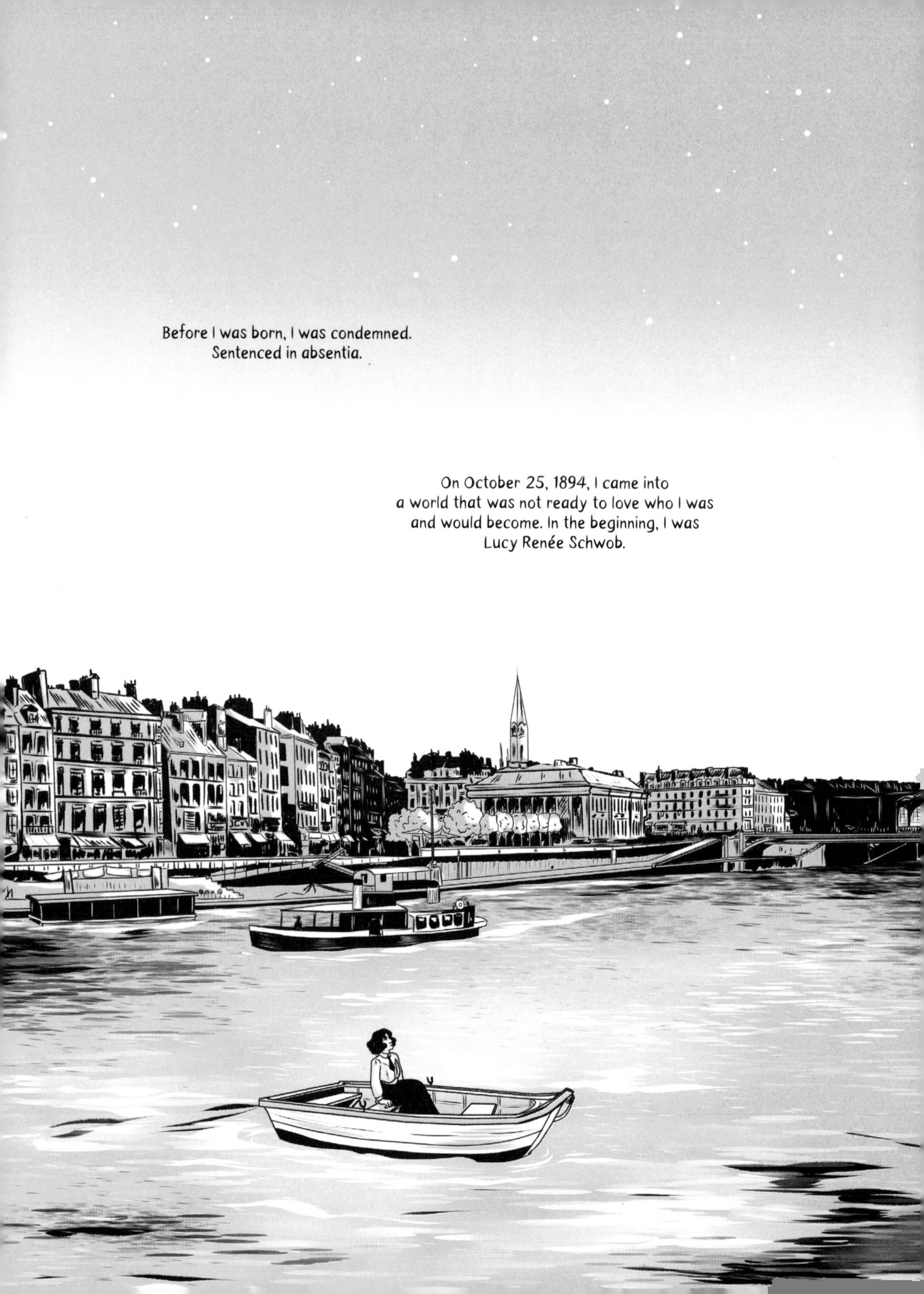
Before I was born, I was condemned. Sentenced in absentia.
On October 25, 1894, I came into a world that was not ready to love who I was and would become. In the beginning, I was Lucy Renée Schwob.

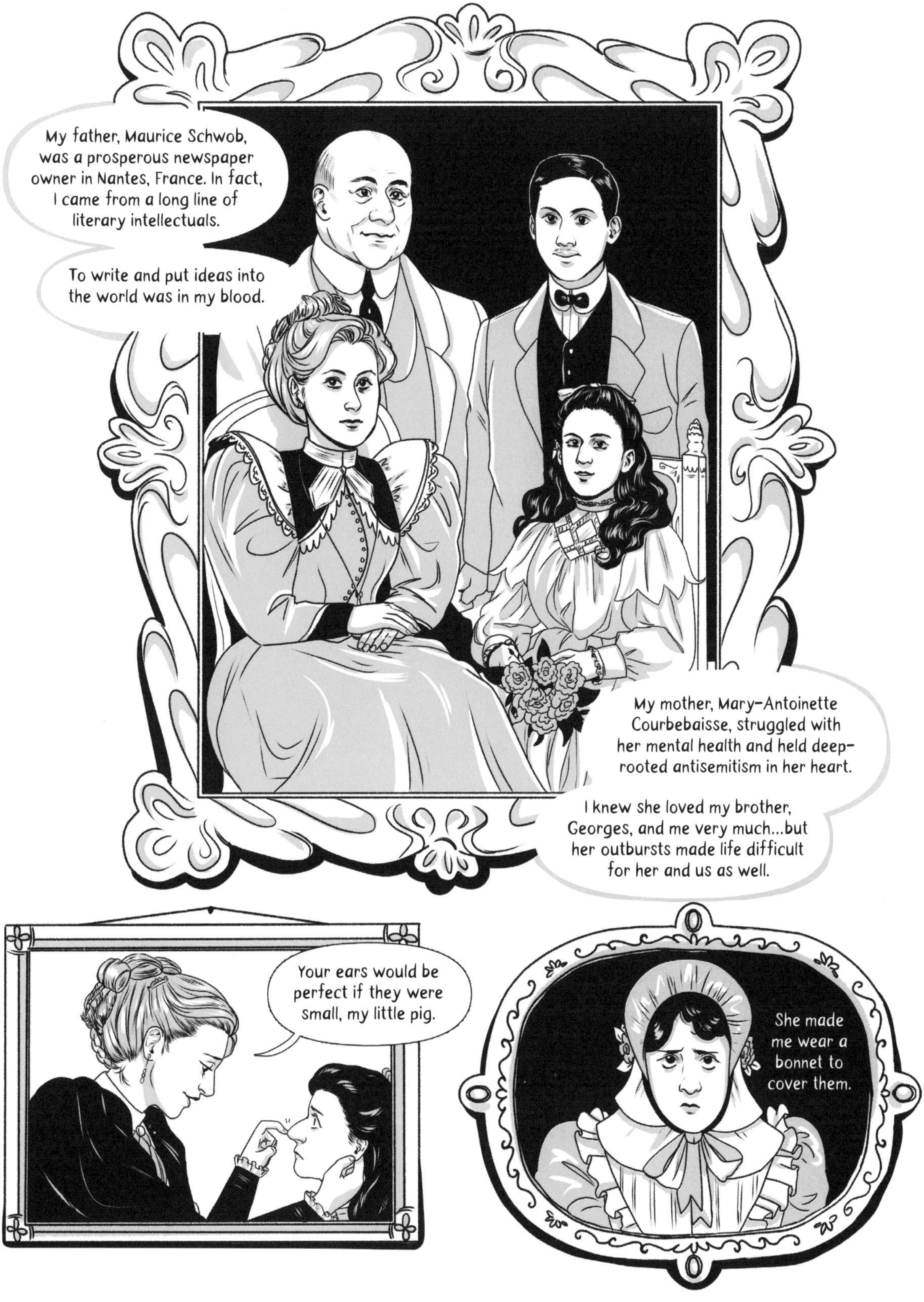
My father, Maurice Schwob, was a prosperous newspaper owner in Nantes, France. In fact, I came from a long line of literary intellectuals.
To write and put ideas into the world was in my blood.
My mother, Mary-Antoinette Courbebaisse, struggled with her mental health and held deep-rooted antisemitism in her heart.
I knew she loved my brother, Georges, and me very much...but her outbursts made life difficult for her and us as well.
Your ears would be perfect if they were small, my little pig.
She made me wear a bonnet to cover them.

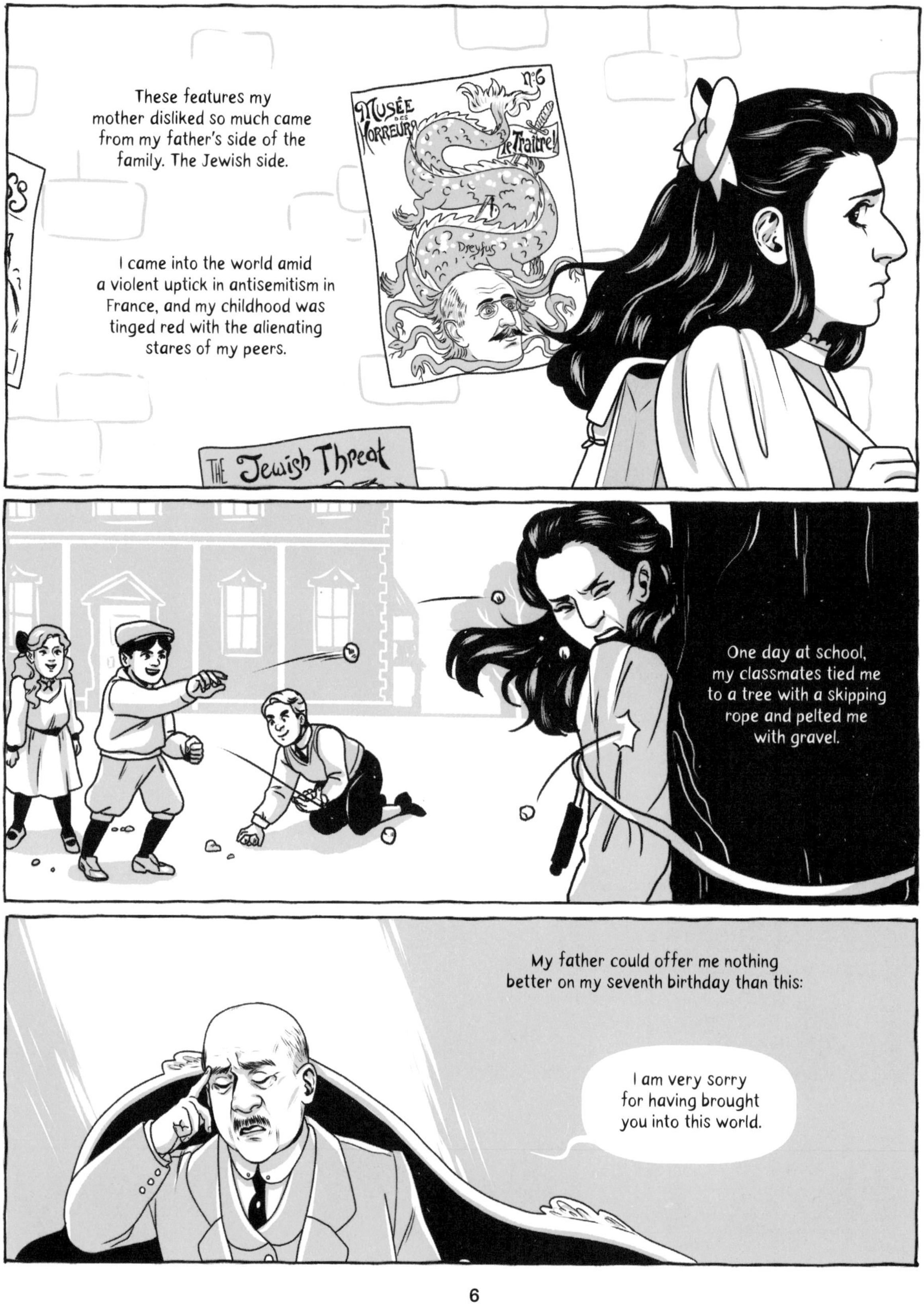
These features my mother disliked so much came from my father's side of the family. The Jewish side.
MUSÉE DES HORREURS
N°6
Le Traître!
Dreyfus
I came into the world amid a violent uptick in antisemitism in France, and my childhood was tinged red with the alienating stares of my peers.
THE Jewish Threat
One day at school, my classmates tied me to a tree with a skipping rope and pelted me with gravel.
My father could offer me nothing better on my seventh birthday than this:
I am very sorry for having brought you into this world.

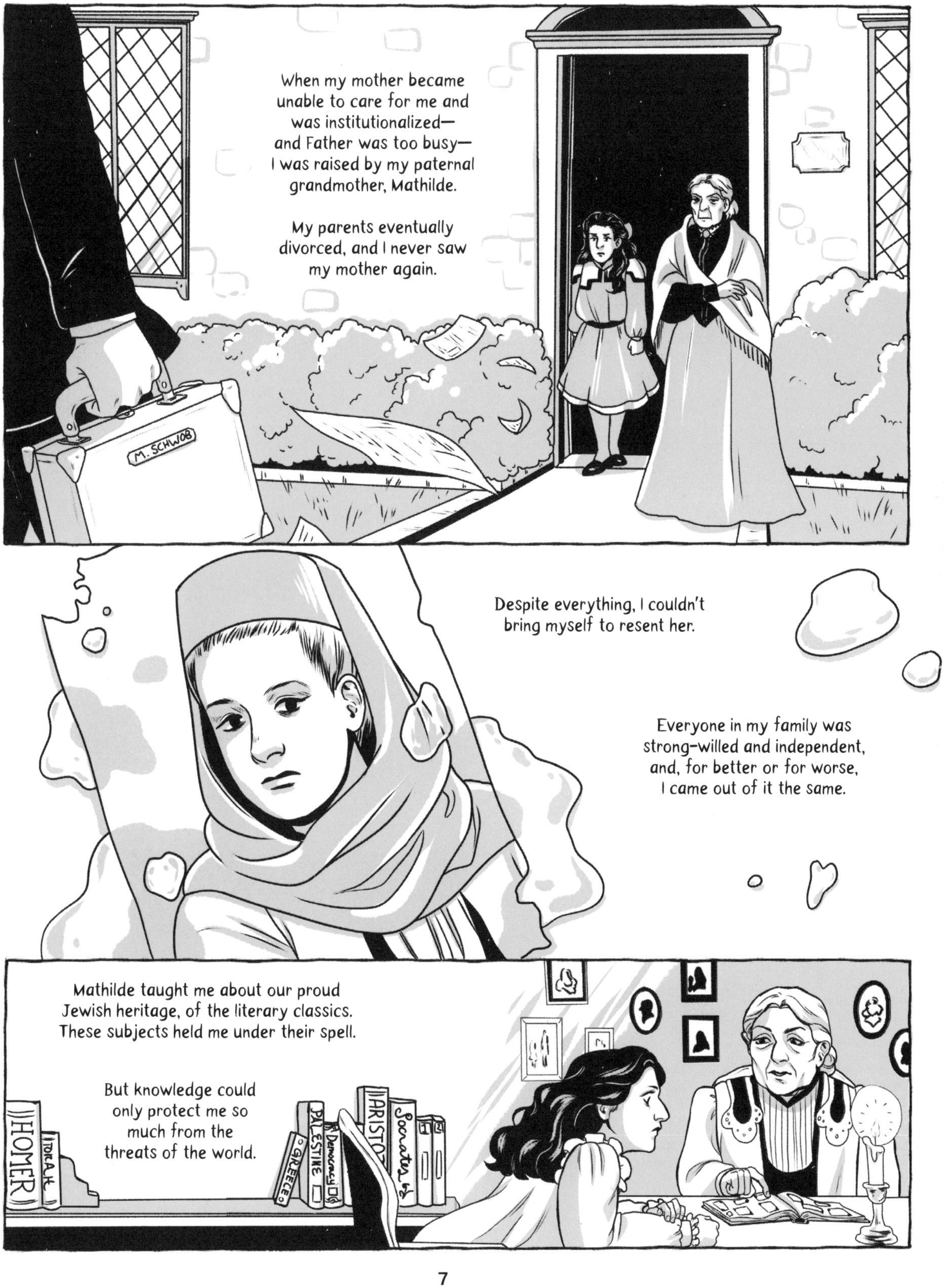
When my mother became unable to care for me and was institutionalized— and Father was too busy— I was raised by my paternal grandmother, Mathilde.
My parents eventually divorced, and I never saw my mother again.
M. SCHWOB
Despite everything, I couldn't bring myself to resent her.
Everyone in my family was strong-willed and independent, and, for better or for worse, I came out of it the same.
Mathilde taught me about our proud Jewish heritage, of the literary classics. These subjects held me under their spell.
But knowledge could only protect me so much from the threats of the world.
HOMER
TORAH
GREECE
PALESTINE
Democracy
ARISTO
Socrates

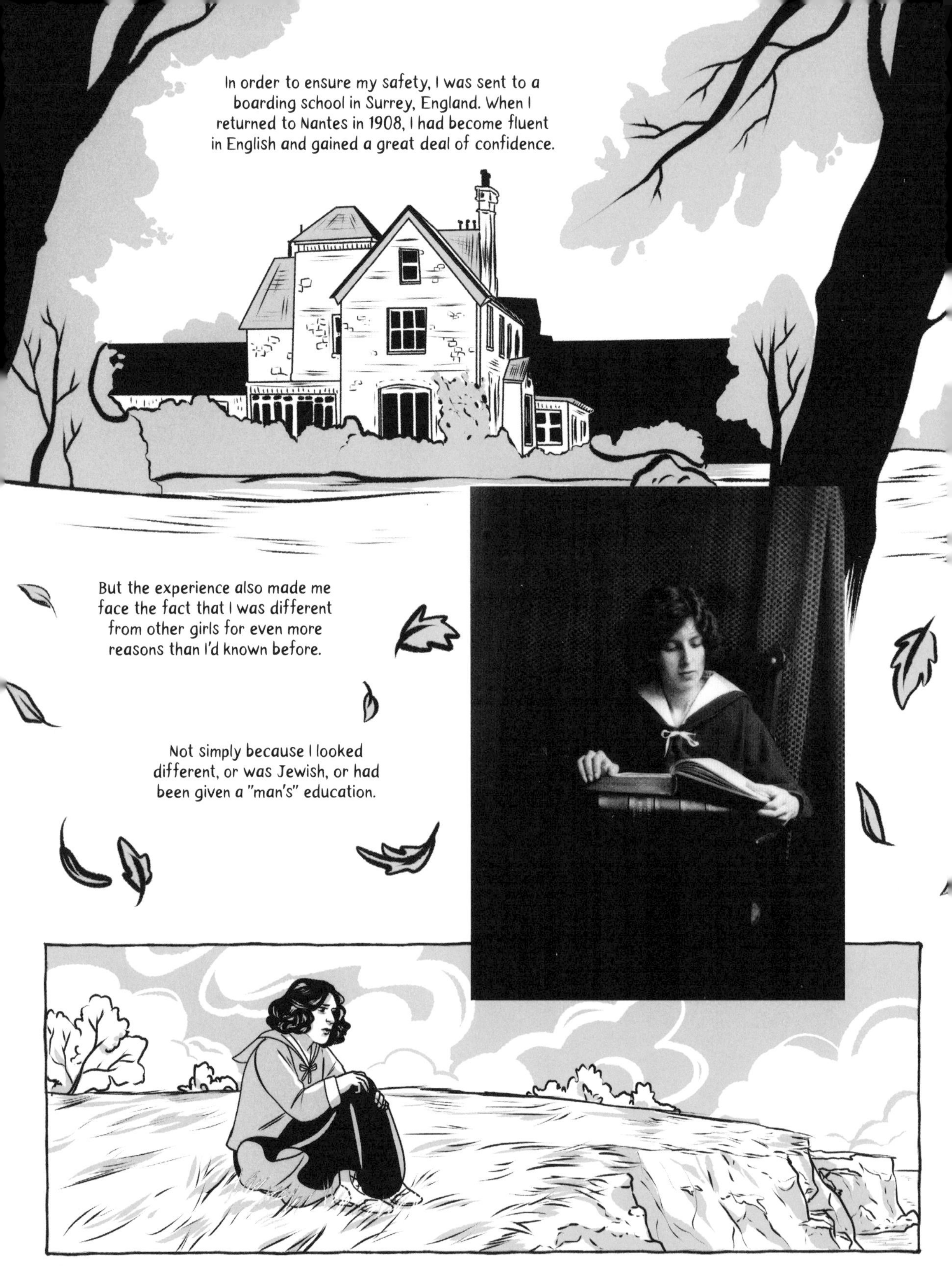
In order to ensure my safety, I was sent to a boarding school in Surrey, England. When I returned to Nantes in 1908, I had become fluent in English and gained a great deal of confidence.
But the experience also made me face the fact that I was different from other girls for even more reasons than I'd known before.
Not simply because I looked different, or was Jewish, or had been given a "man's" education.

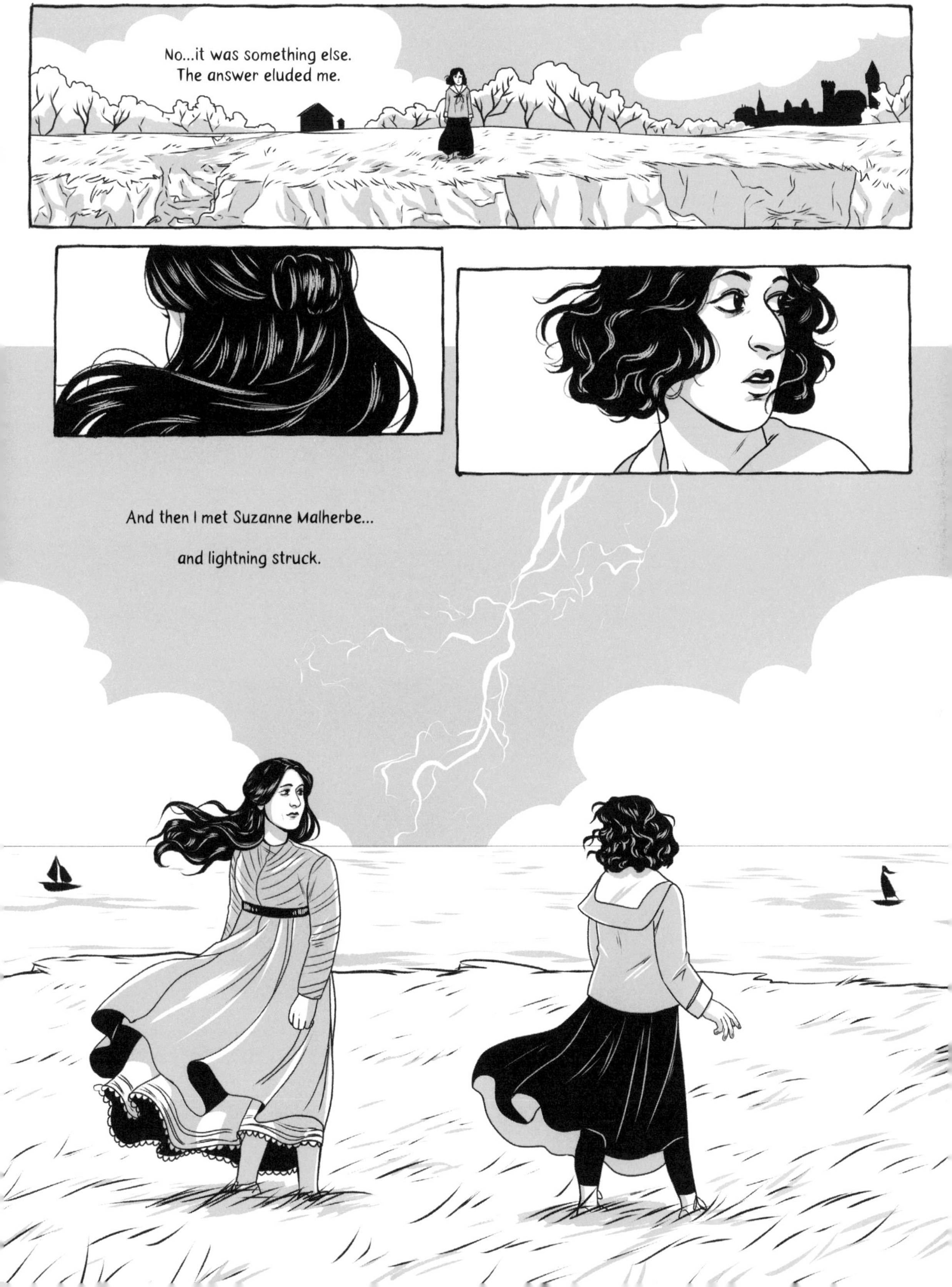
No...it was something else.
The answer eluded me.
And then I met Suzanne Malherbe...
and lightning struck.

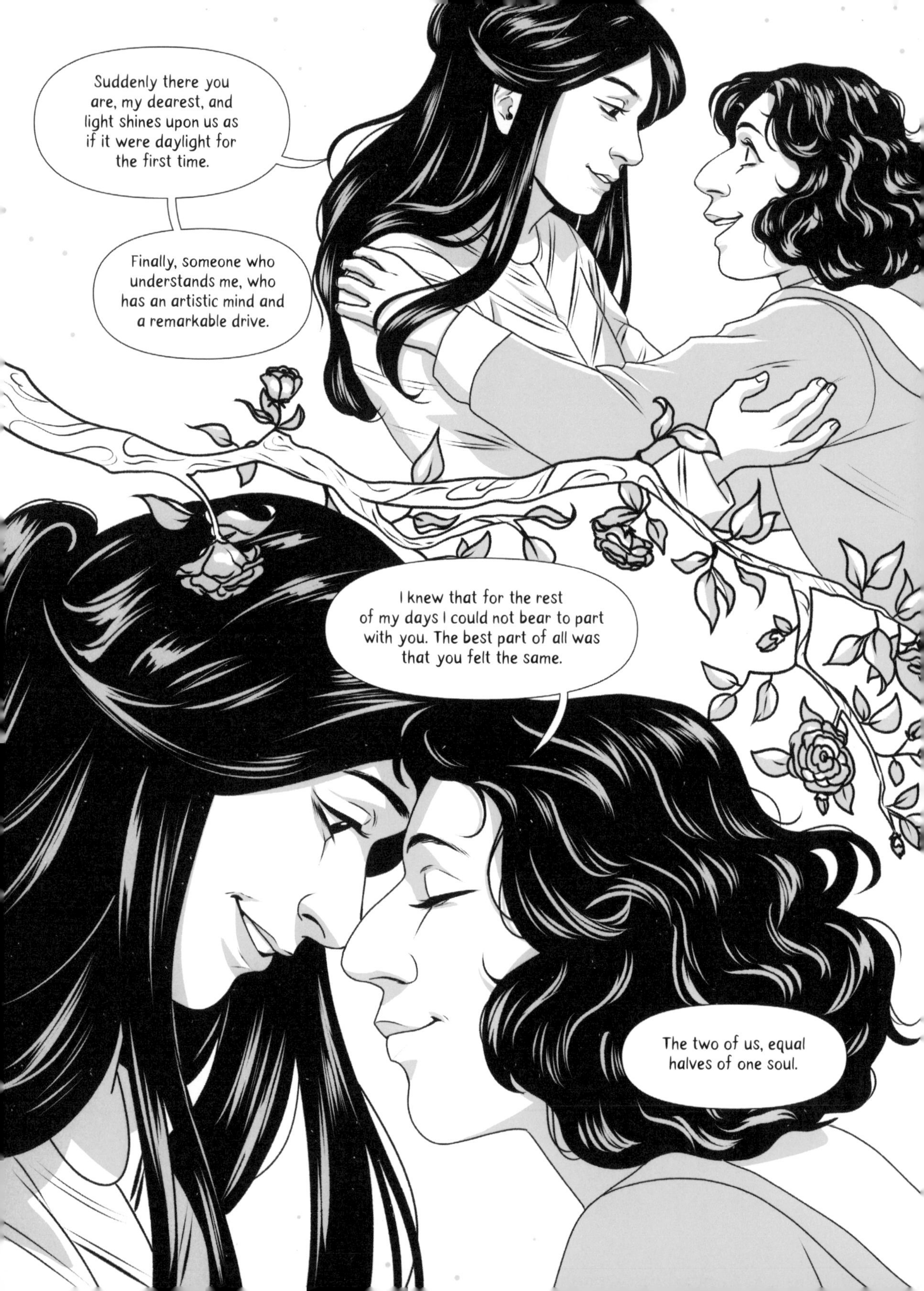
Suddenly there you are, my dearest, and light shines upon us as if it were daylight for the first time.
Finally, someone who understands me, who has an artistic mind and a remarkable drive.
I knew that for the rest of my days I could not bear to part with you. The best part of all was that you felt the same.
The two of us, equal halves of one soul.

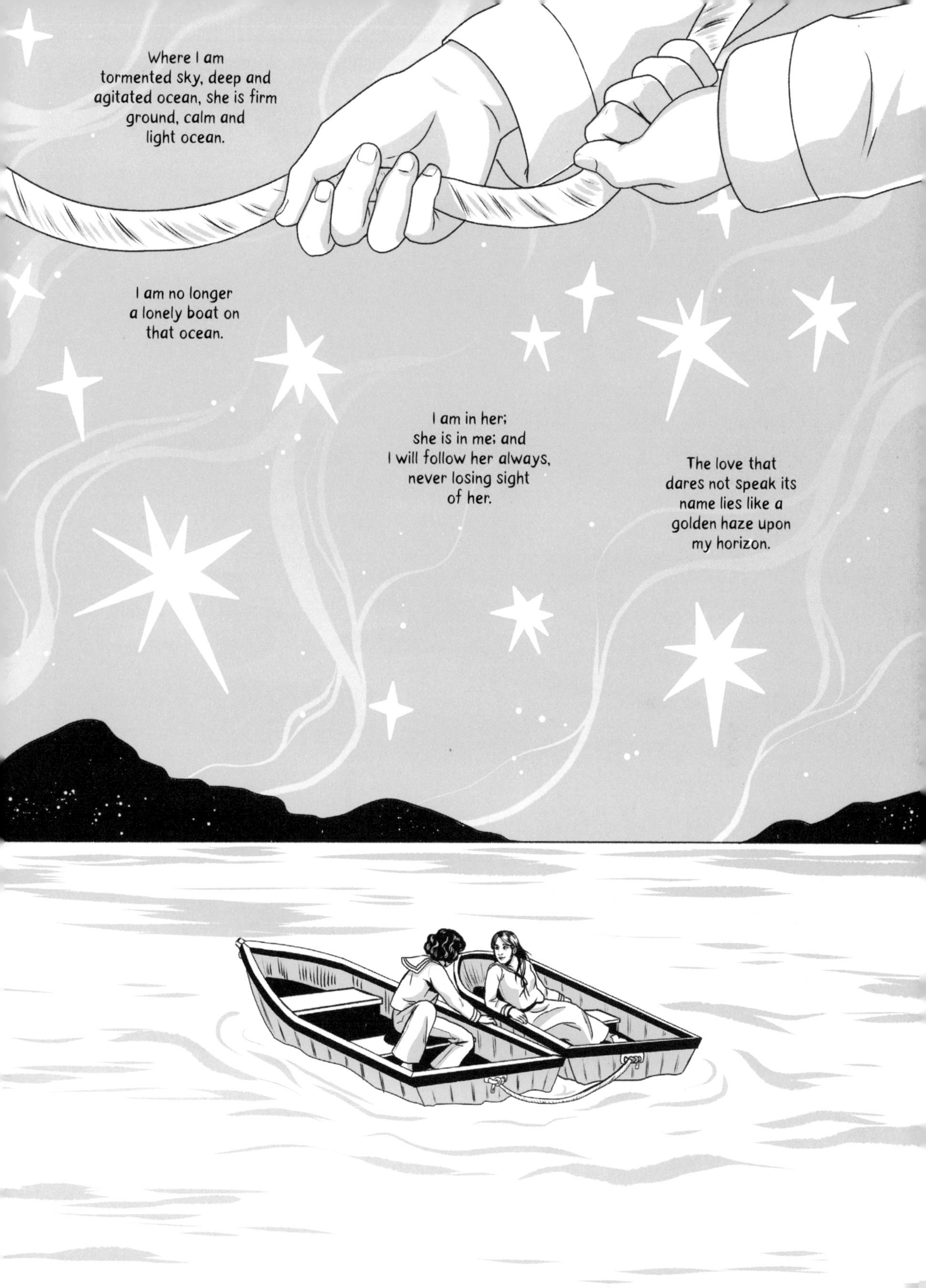
Where I am tormented sky, deep and agitated ocean, she is firm ground, calm and light ocean.
I am no longer a lonely boat on that ocean.
I am in her; she is in me; and I will follow her always, never losing sight of her.
The love that dares not speak its name lies like a golden haze upon my horizon.

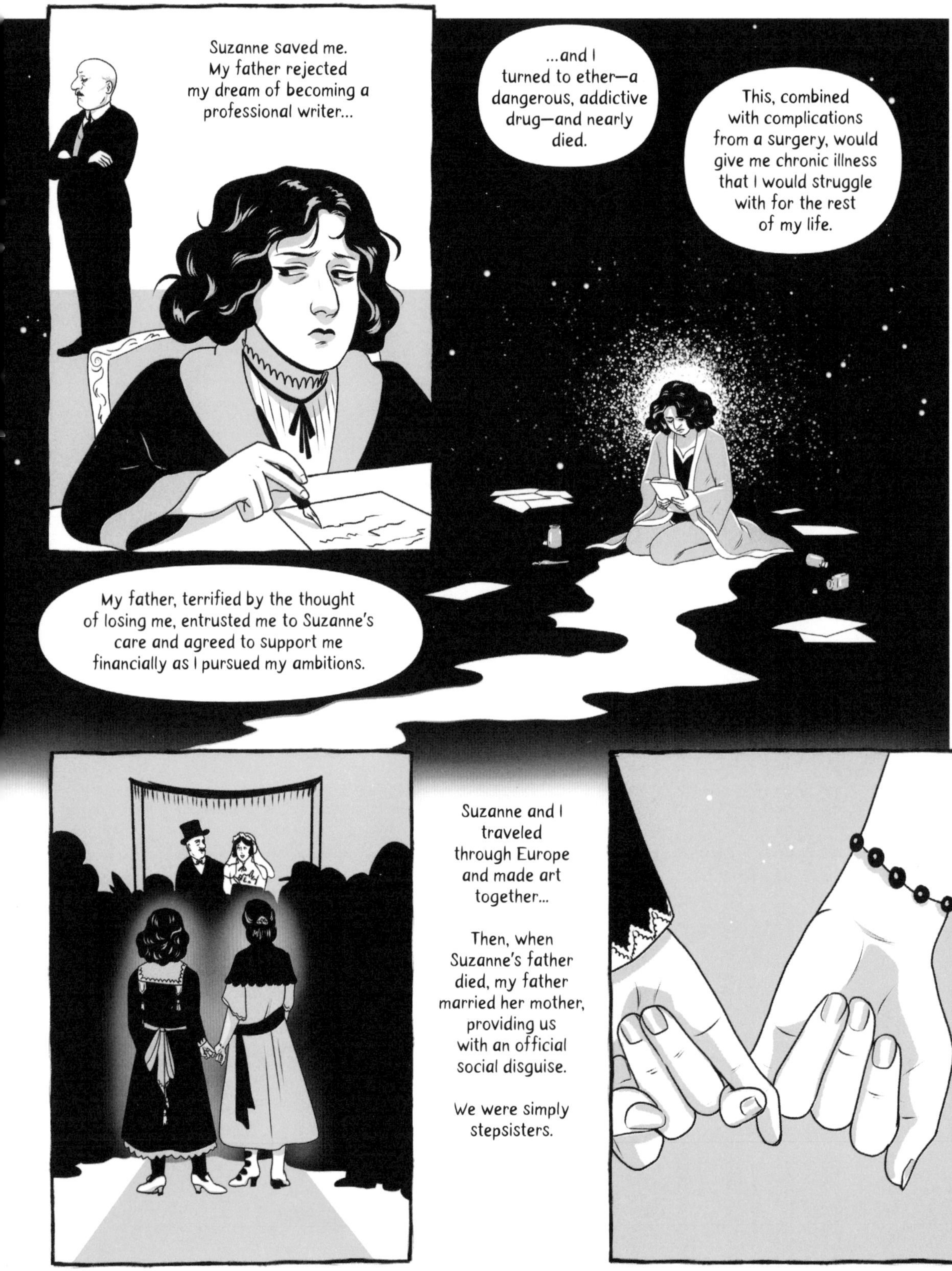
Suzanne saved me. My father rejected my dream of becoming a professional writer...
...and I turned to ether—a dangerous, addictive drug—and nearly died.
This, combined with complications from a surgery, would give me chronic illness that I would struggle with for the rest of my life.
My father, terrified by the thought of losing me, entrusted me to Suzanne's care and agreed to support me financially as I pursued my ambitions.
Suzanne and I traveled through Europe and made art together...
Then, when Suzanne's father died, my father married her mother, providing us with an official social disguise.
We were simply stepsisters.

But these years, full of warmth from young love, were also tainted by war and social unrest.

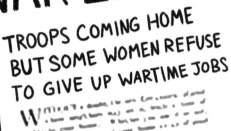

Le Parisien

5 cent   5 cent   5 cent

Lundi, 11 Novembre 1918

THE WAR ENDS!

MASCULINE WOMEN? FEMININE MEN?

TROOPS COMING HOME BUT SOME WOMEN REFUSE TO GIVE UP WARTIME JOBS

W

THE JEWISH QUESTION

—OBITUARIES—

When the ash, smoke, and mustard gas finally cleared, everyone on the continent had to figure out how to move on and live.

I had only recently regained a chance at life. Now I had the rest of it to figure out who I truly was.

Le Parisien

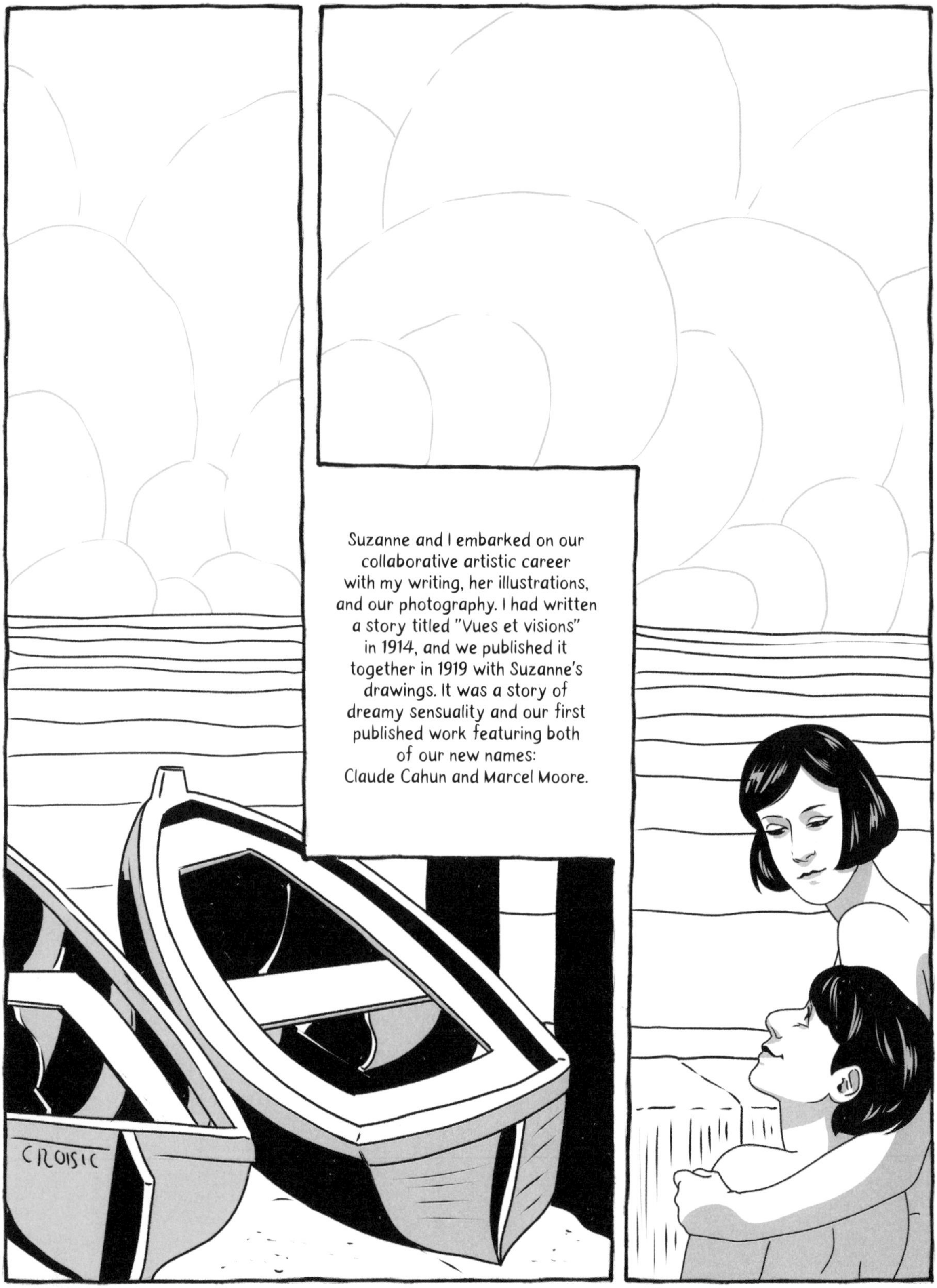

Suzanne and I embarked on our collaborative artistic career with my writing, her illustrations, and our photography. I had written a story titled "Vues et visions" in 1914, and we published it together in 1919 with Suzanne's drawings. It was a story of dreamy sensuality and our first published work featuring both of our new names: Claude Cahun and Marcel Moore.
CROISIC

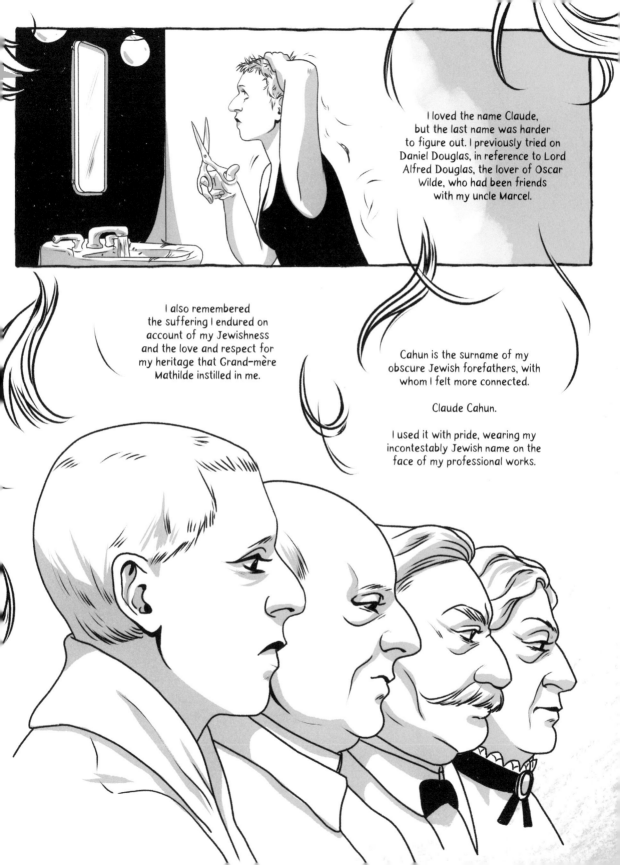

I loved the name Claude, but the last name was harder to figure out. I previously tried on Daniel Douglas, in reference to Lord Alfred Douglas, the lover of Oscar Wilde, who had been friends with my uncle Marcel.

I also remembered the suffering I endured on account of my Jewishness and the love and respect for my heritage that Grand-mère Mathilde instilled in me.

Cahun is the surname of my obscure Jewish forefathers, with whom I felt more connected.

Claude Cahun.

I used it with pride, wearing my incontestably Jewish name on the face of my professional works.

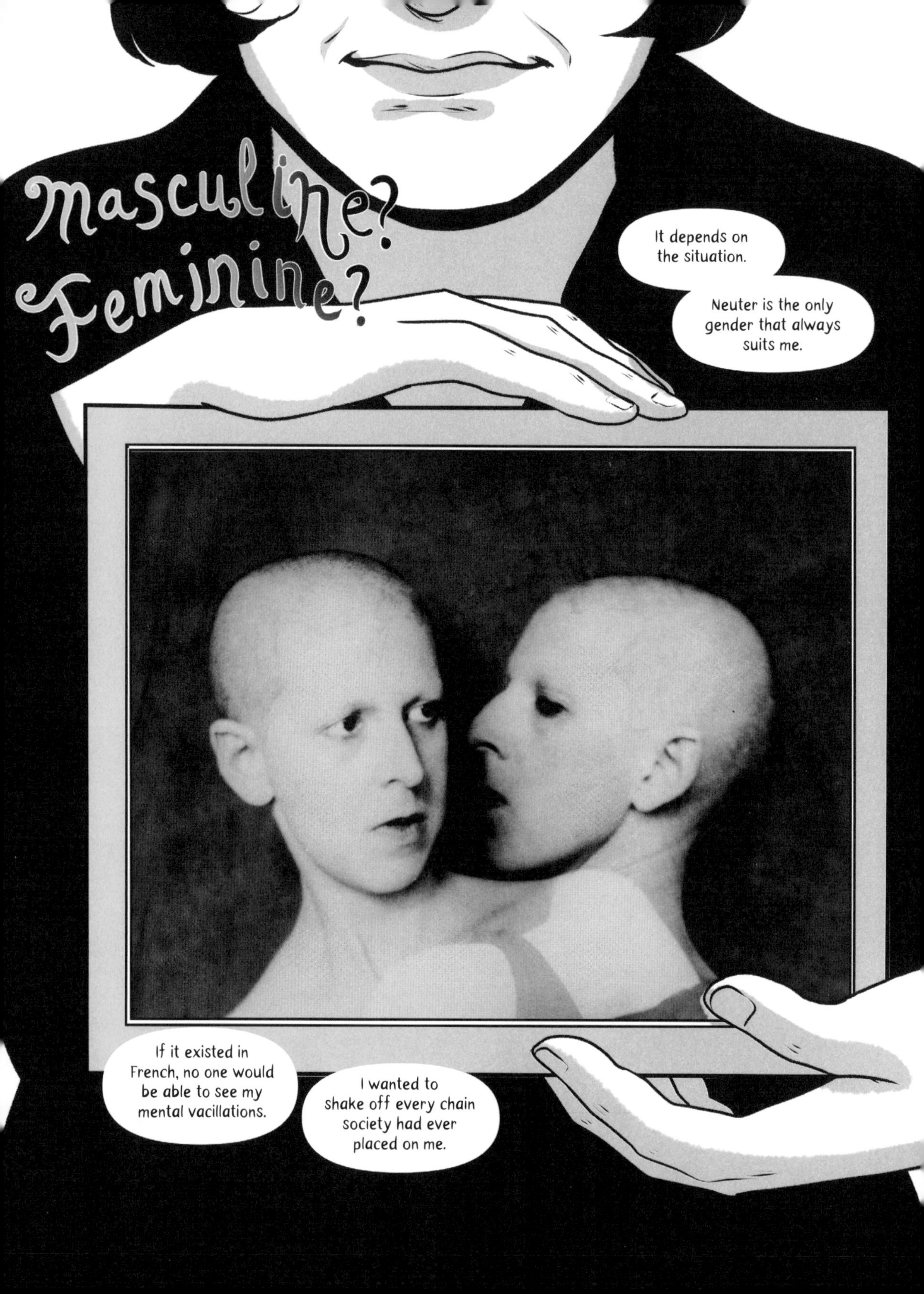
Masculine?
Feminine?
It depends on the situation.
Neuter is the only gender that always suits me.
If it existed in French, no one would be able to see my mental vacillations.
I wanted to shake off every chain society had ever placed on me.

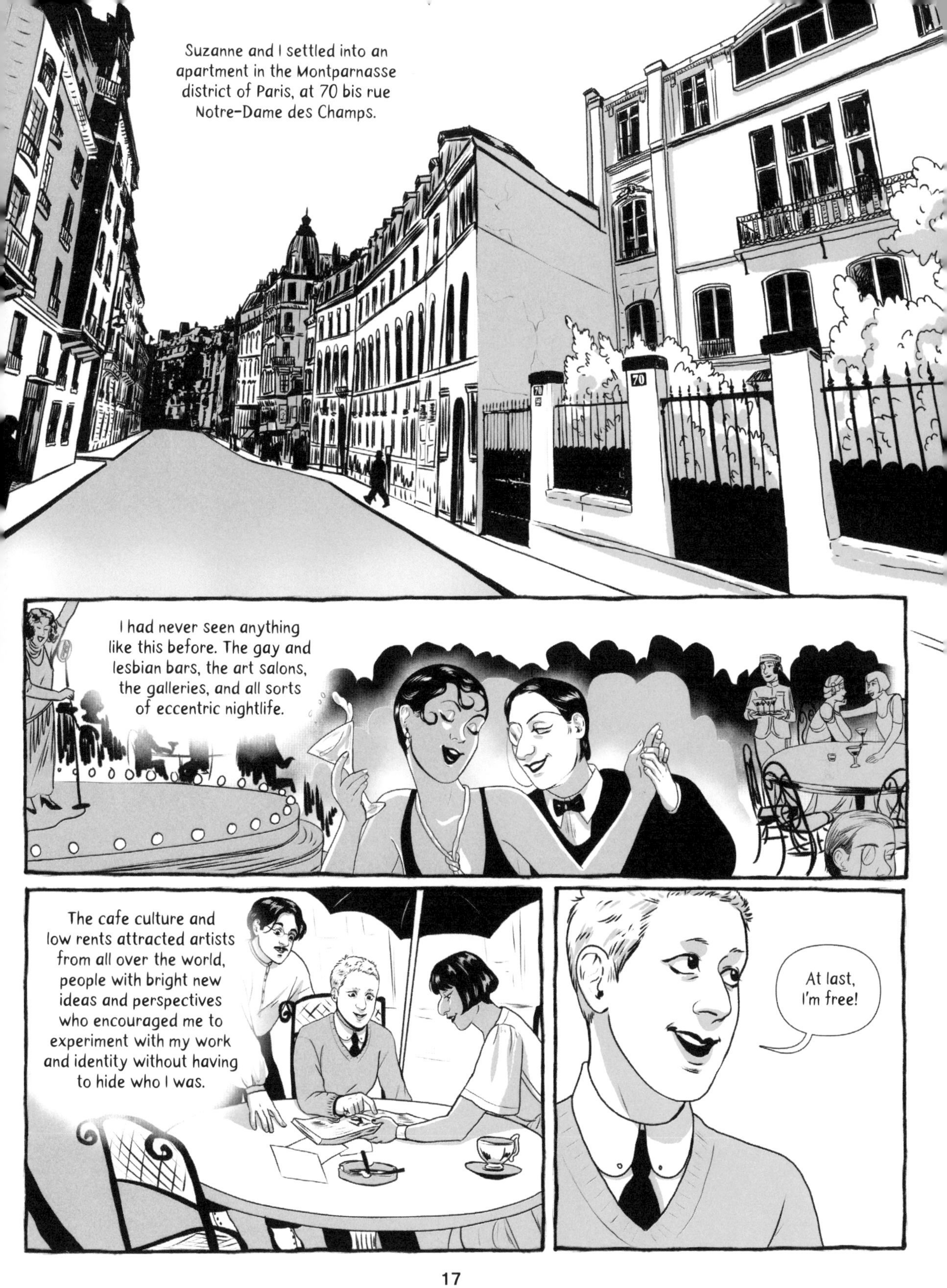
Suzanne and I settled into an apartment in the Montparnasse district of Paris, at 70 bis rue Notre-Dame des Champs.
70
70
I had never seen anything like this before. The gay and lesbian bars, the art salons, the galleries, and all sorts of eccentric nightlife.
The cafe culture and low rents attracted artists from all over the world, people with bright new ideas and perspectives who encouraged me to experiment with my work and identity without having to hide who I was.
At last, I'm free!

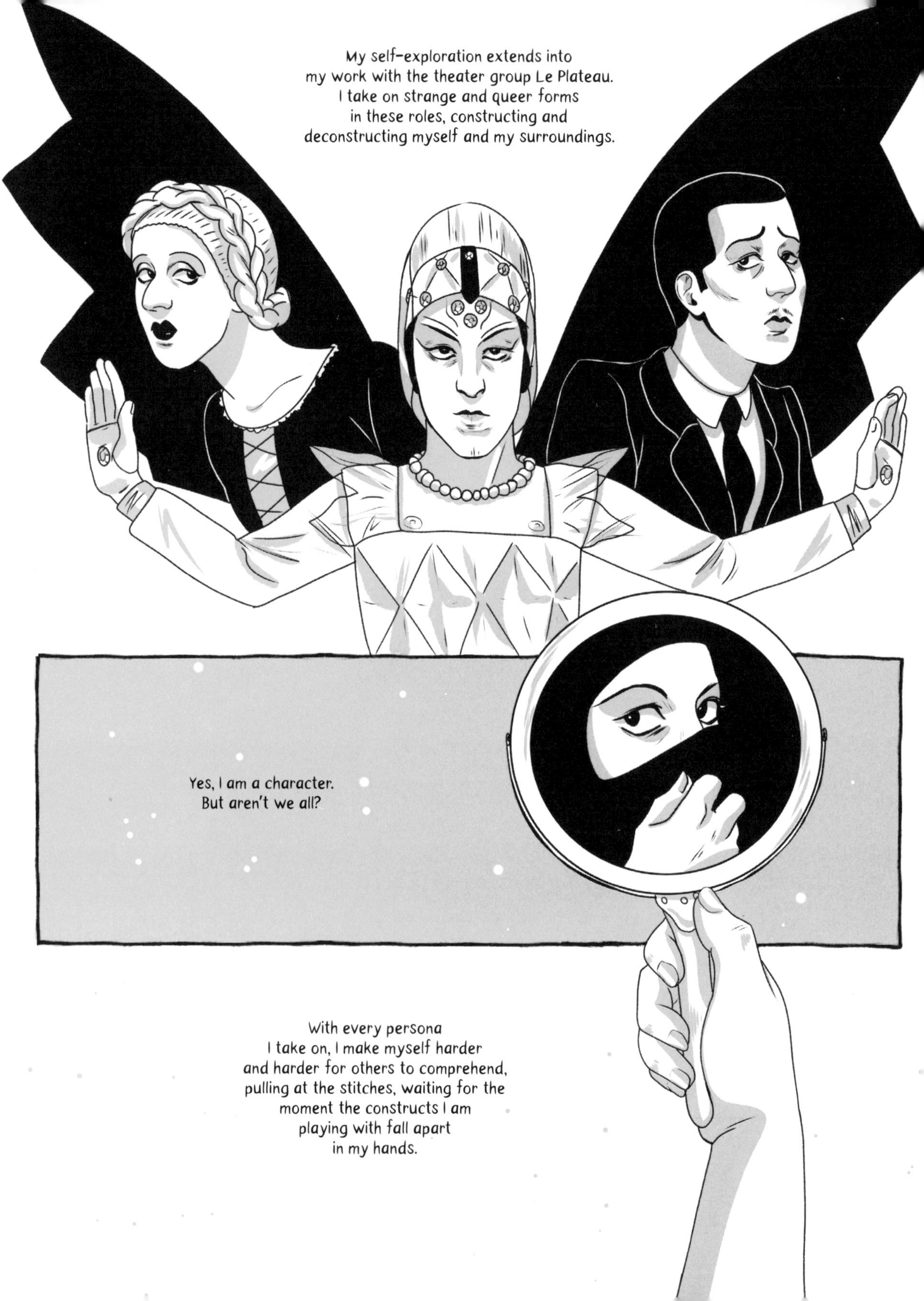
My self-exploration extends into my work with the theater group Le Plateau. I take on strange and queer forms in these roles, constructing and deconstructing myself and my surroundings.
Yes, I am a character. But aren't we all?
With every persona I take on, I make myself harder and harder for others to comprehend, pulling at the stitches, waiting for the moment the constructs I am playing with fall apart in my hands.

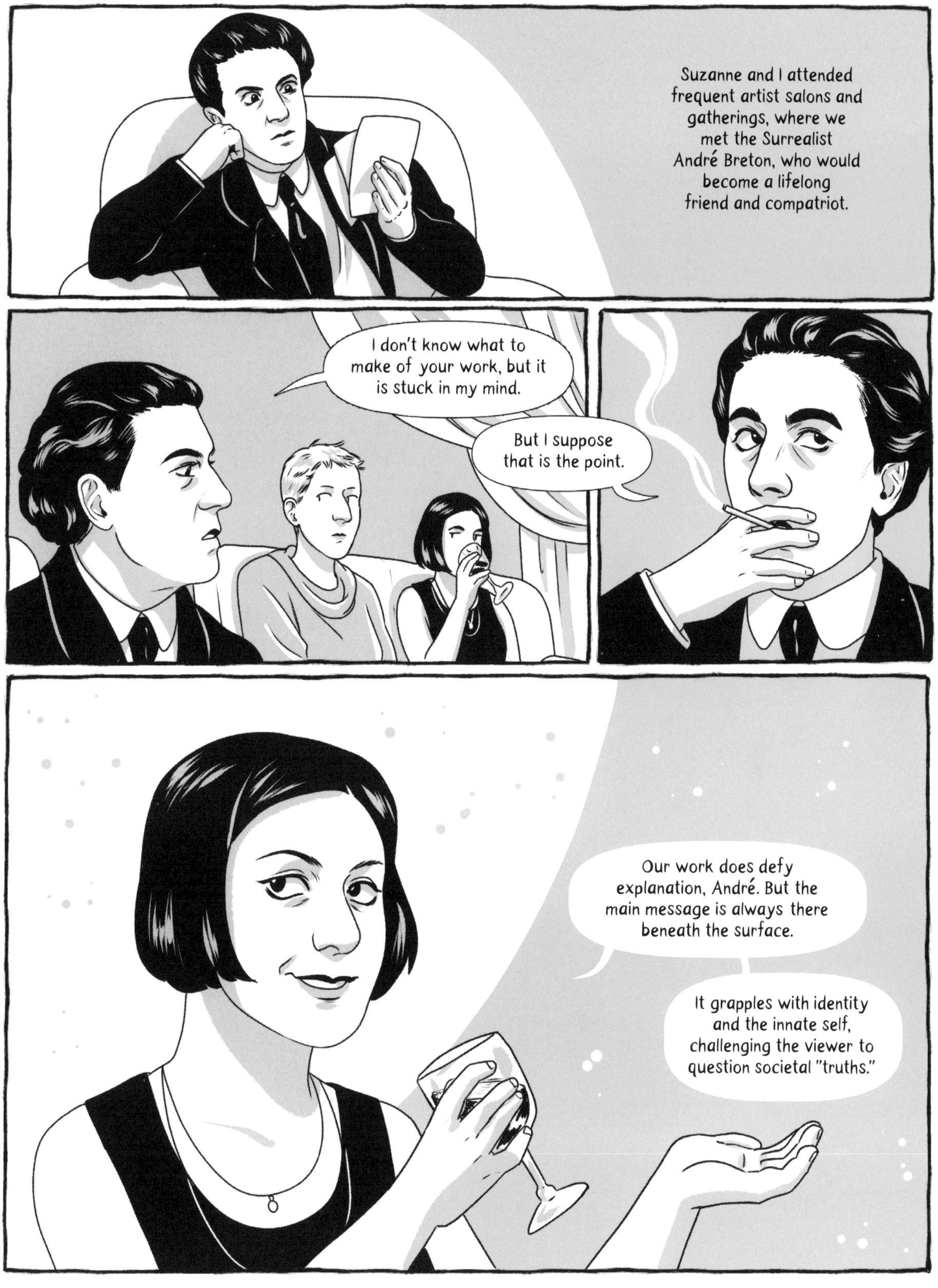
Suzanne and I attended frequent artist salons and gatherings, where we met the Surrealist André Breton, who would become a lifelong friend and compatriot.
I don't know what to make of your work, but it is stuck in my mind.
But I suppose that is the point.
Our work does defy explanation, André. But the main message is always there beneath the surface.
It grapples with identity and the innate self, challenging the viewer to question societal "truths."

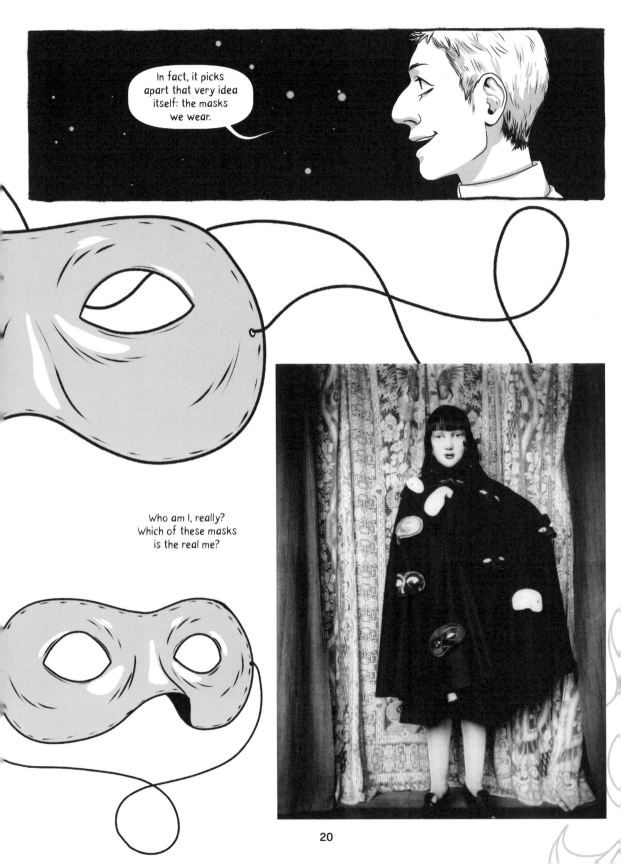

In fact, it picks apart that very idea itself: the masks we wear.

Who am I, really? Which of these masks is the real me?

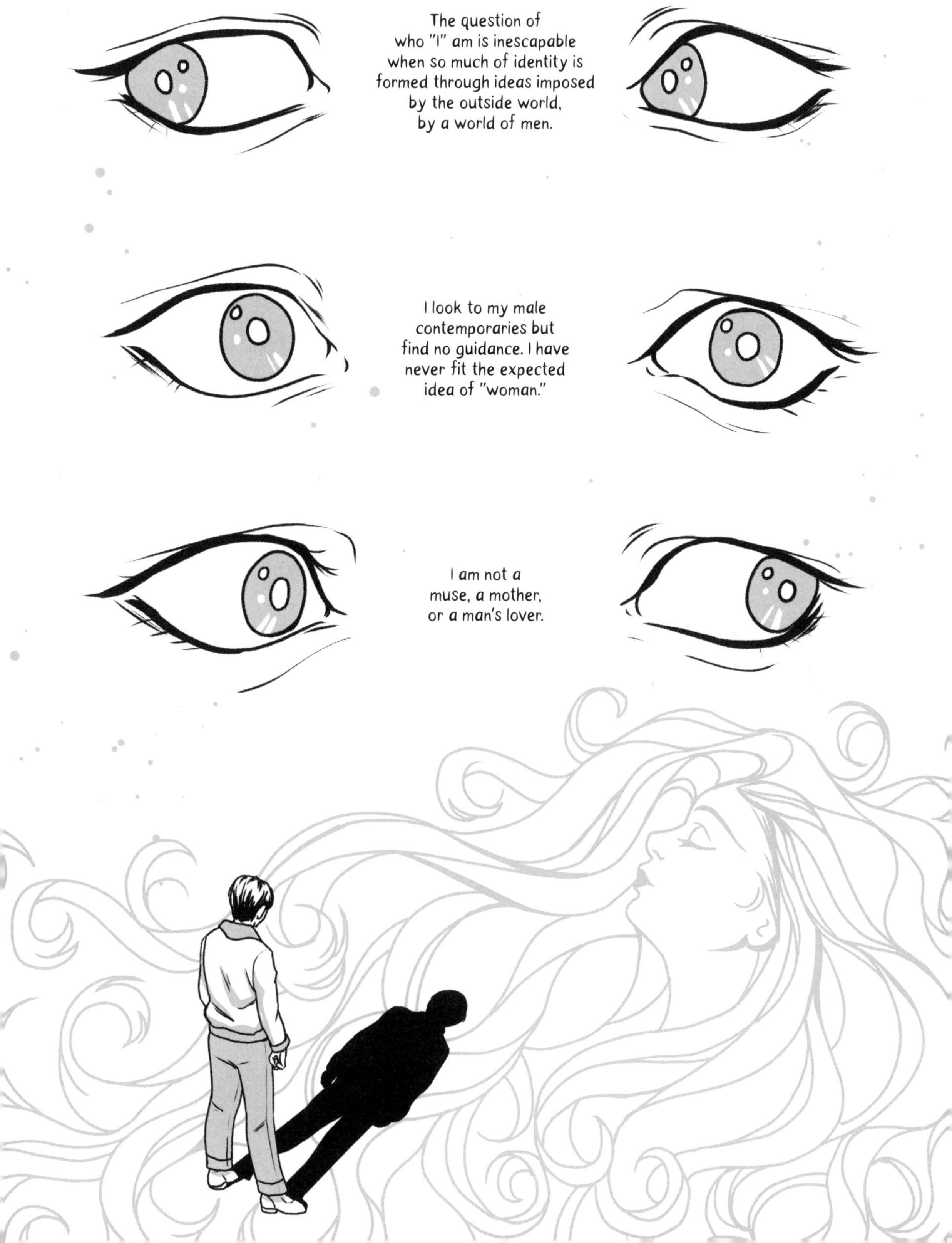
The question of who "I" am is inescapable when so much of identity is formed through ideas imposed by the outside world, by a world of men.
I look to my male contemporaries but find no guidance. I have never fit the expected idea of "woman."
I am not a muse, a mother, or a man's lover.

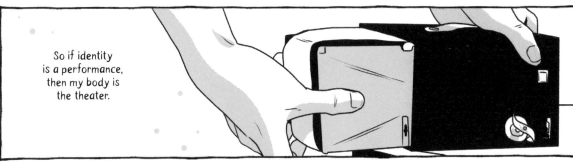

So if identity
is a performance,
then my body is
the theater.

I put on a mask,
I take one off.
Under this mask,
there is another
mask. I will never
finish removing
these faces.

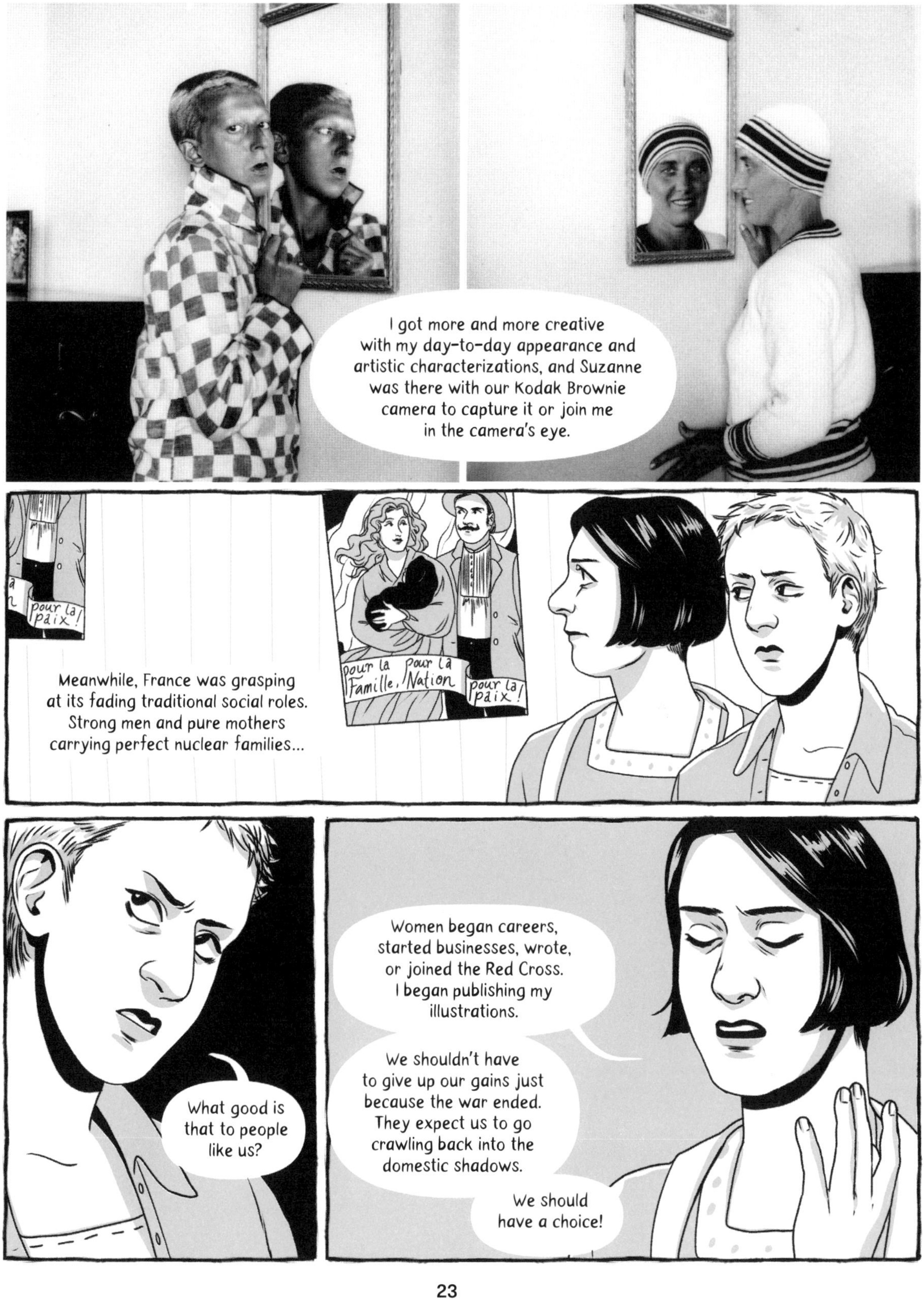
I got more and more creative with my day-to-day appearance and artistic characterizations, and Suzanne was there with our Kodak Brownie camera to capture it or join me in the camera's eye.
pour la paix!
pour la Famille,
pour la Nation
pour la paix!
Meanwhile, France was grasping at its fading traditional social roles. Strong men and pure mothers carrying perfect nuclear families...
What good is that to people like us?
Women began careers, started businesses, wrote, or joined the Red Cross. I began publishing my illustrations.
We shouldn't have to give up our gains just because the war ended. They expect us to go crawling back into the domestic shadows.
We should have a choice!

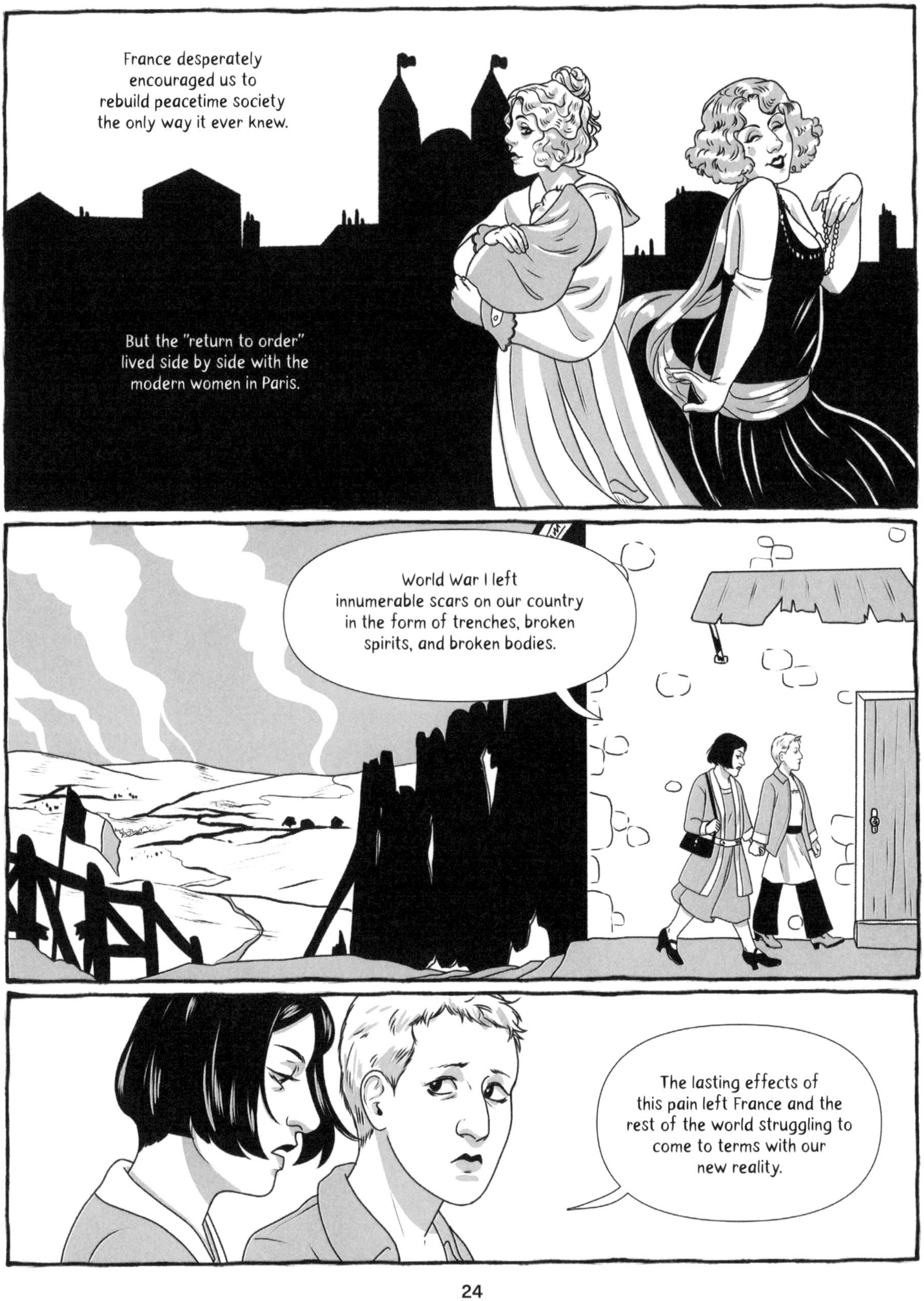
France desperately encouraged us to rebuild peacetime society the only way it ever knew.
But the "return to order" lived side by side with the modern women in Paris.
World War I left innumerable scars on our country in the form of trenches, broken spirits, and broken bodies.
The lasting effects of this pain left France and the rest of the world struggling to come to terms with our new reality.

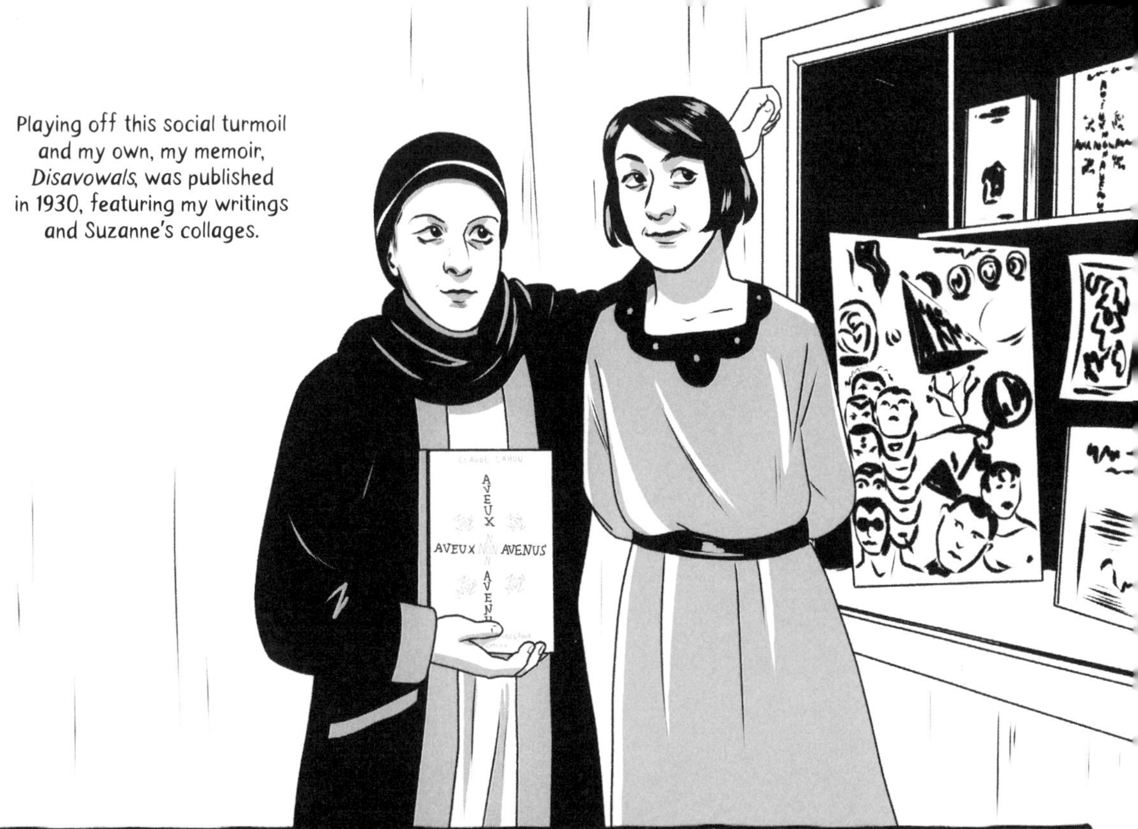
Playing off this social turmoil and my own, my memoir, *Disavowals*, was published in 1930, featuring my writings and Suzanne's collages.
AVEUX NON AVENUS

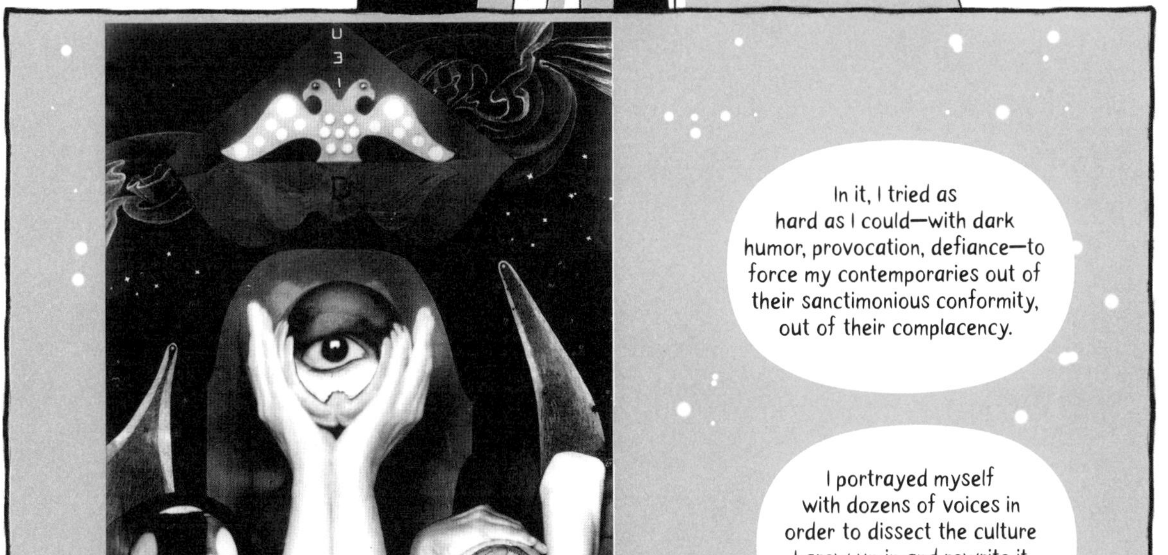
Moore
In it, I tried as hard as I could—with dark humor, provocation, defiance—to force my contemporaries out of their sanctimonious conformity, out of their complacency.
I portrayed myself with dozens of voices in order to dissect the culture I grew up in and rewrite it as something of my own design.

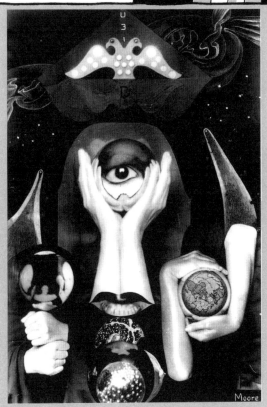

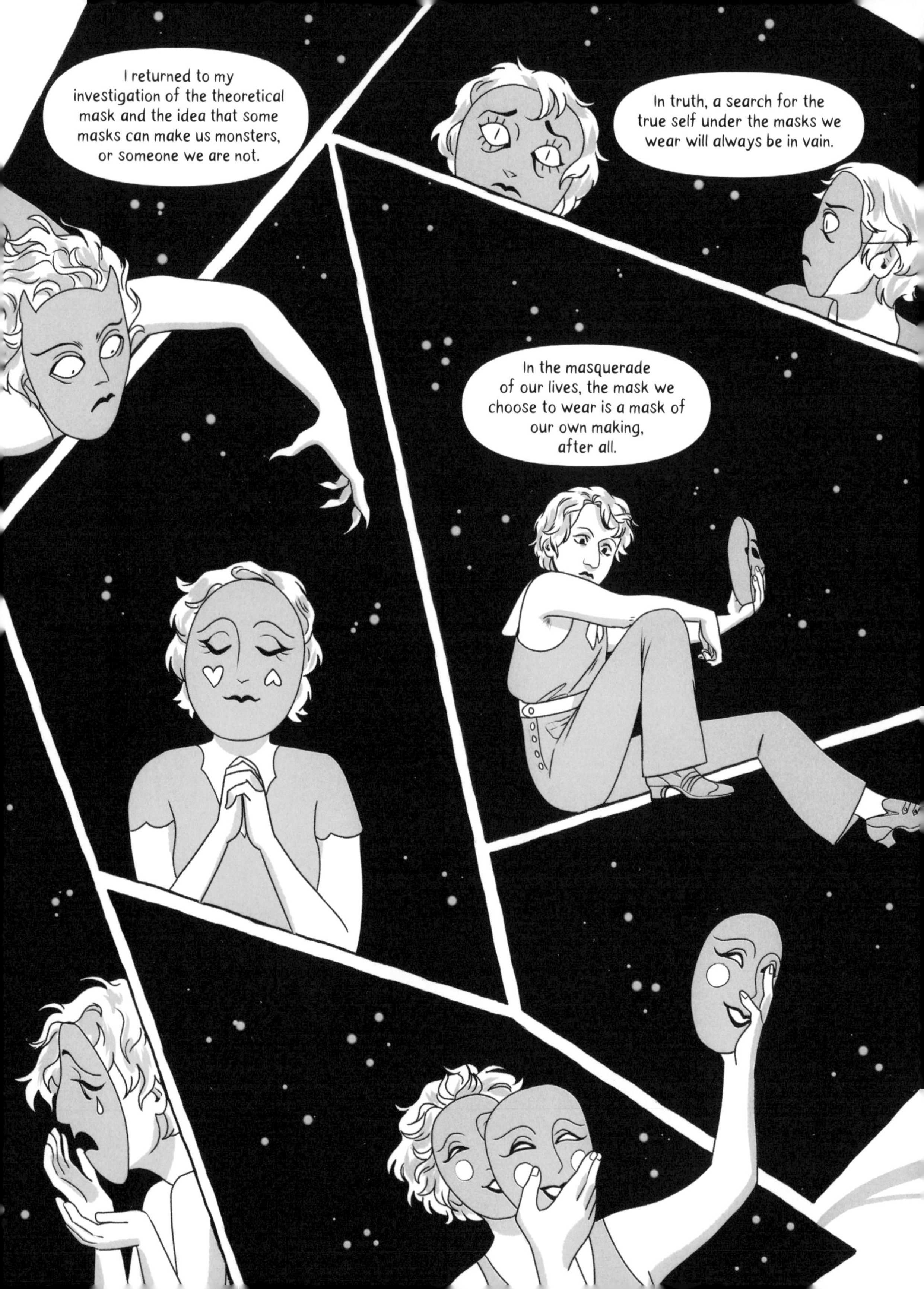
I returned to my investigation of the theoretical mask and the idea that some masks can make us monsters, or someone we are not.
In truth, a search for the true self under the masks we wear will always be in vain.
In the masquerade of our lives, the mask we choose to wear is a mask of our own making, after all.

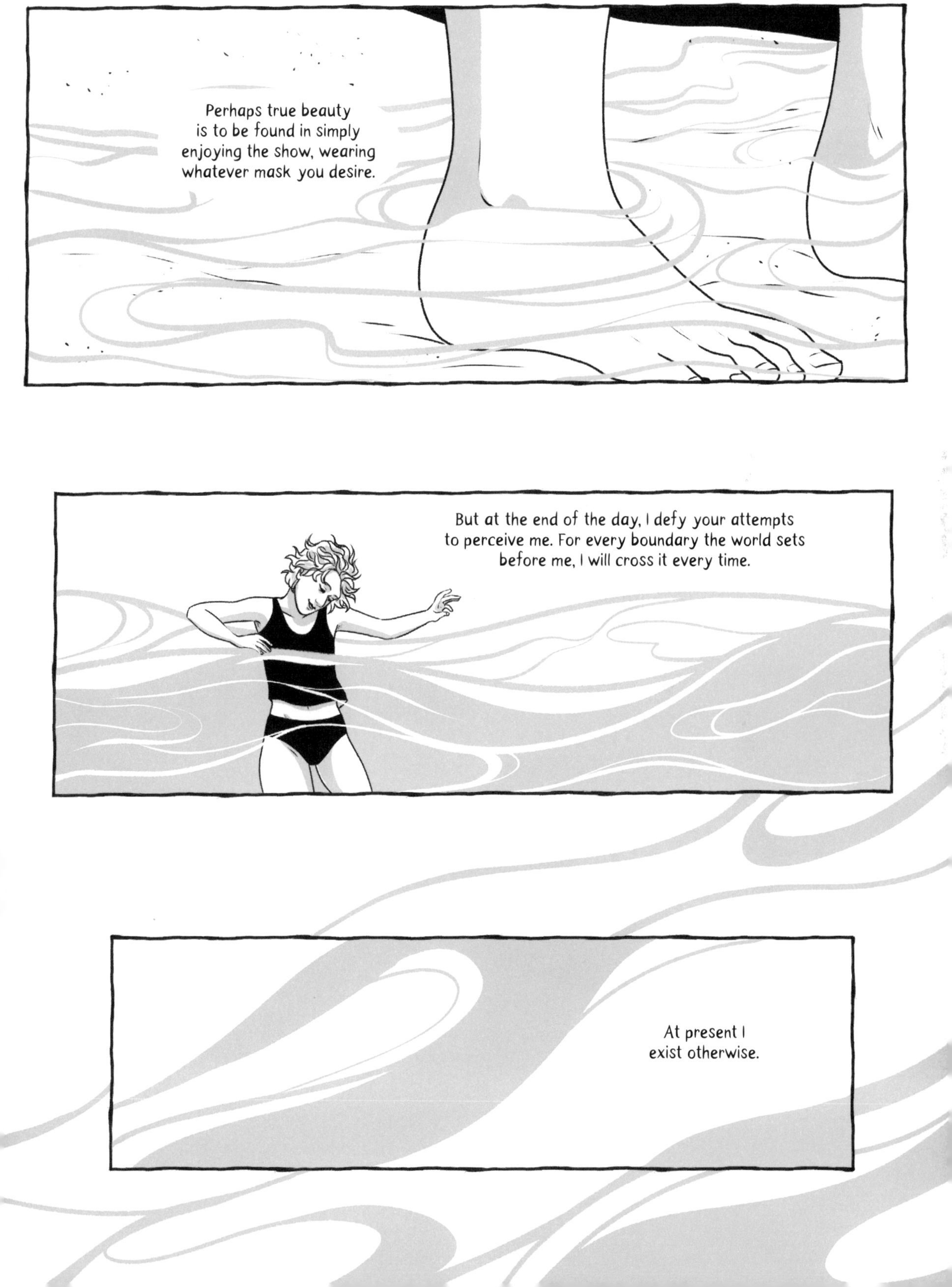
Perhaps true beauty is to be found in simply enjoying the show, wearing whatever mask you desire.
But at the end of the day, I defy your attempts to perceive me. For every boundary the world sets before me, I will cross it every time.
At present I exist otherwise.

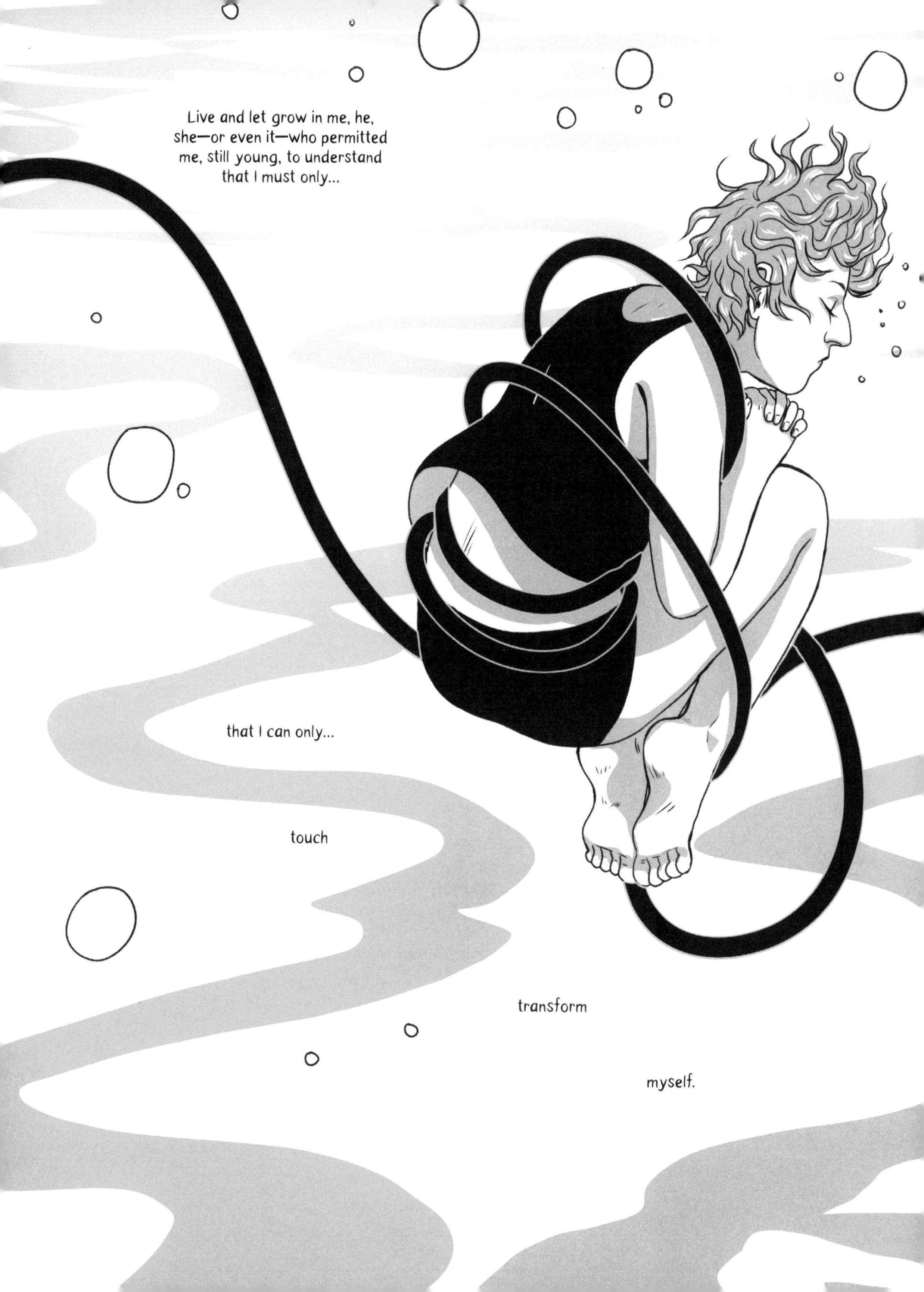
Live and let grow in me, he, she—or even it—who permitted me, still young, to understand that I must only...
that I can only...
touch
transform
myself.

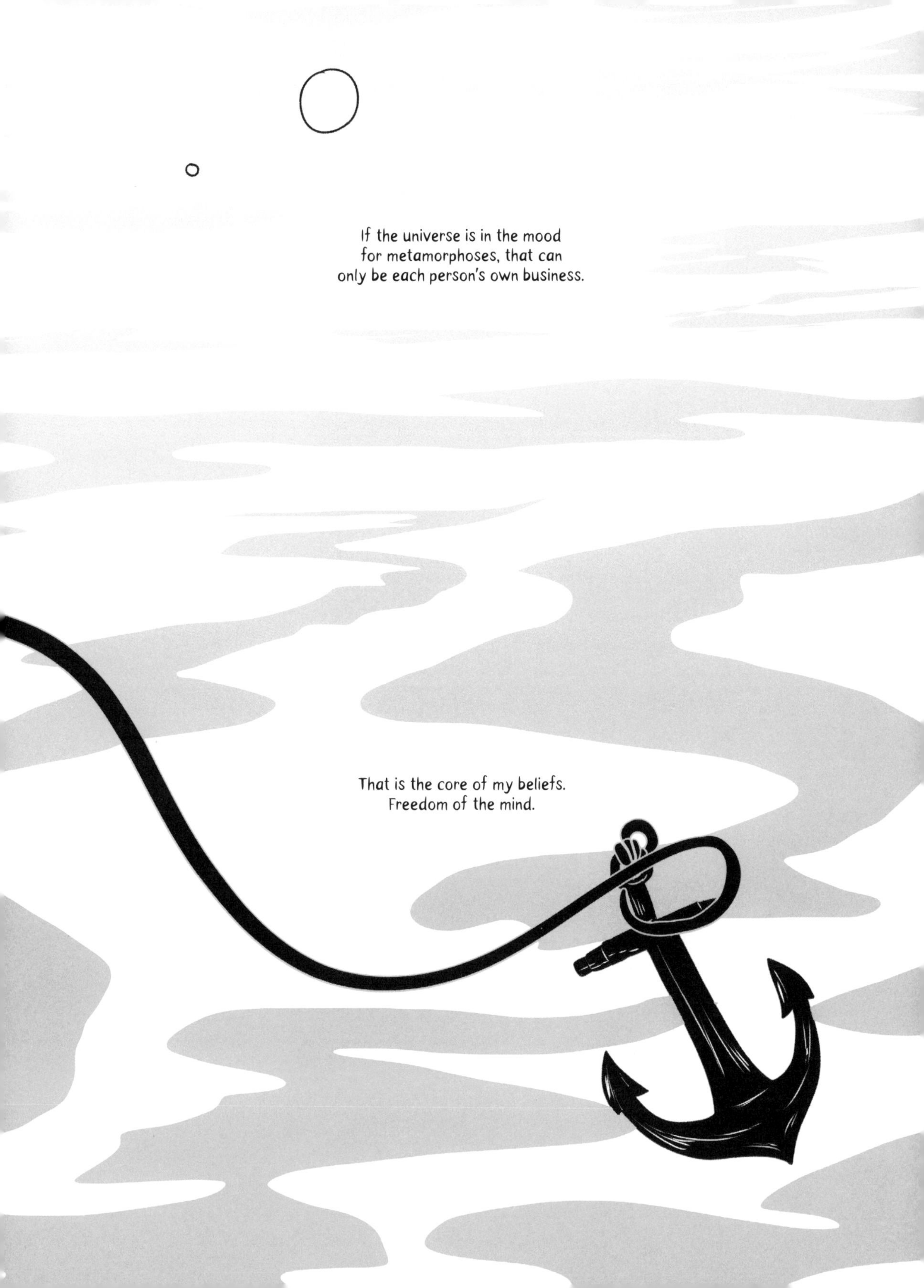
If the universe is in the mood for metamorphoses, that can only be each person's own business.
That is the core of my beliefs. Freedom of the mind.

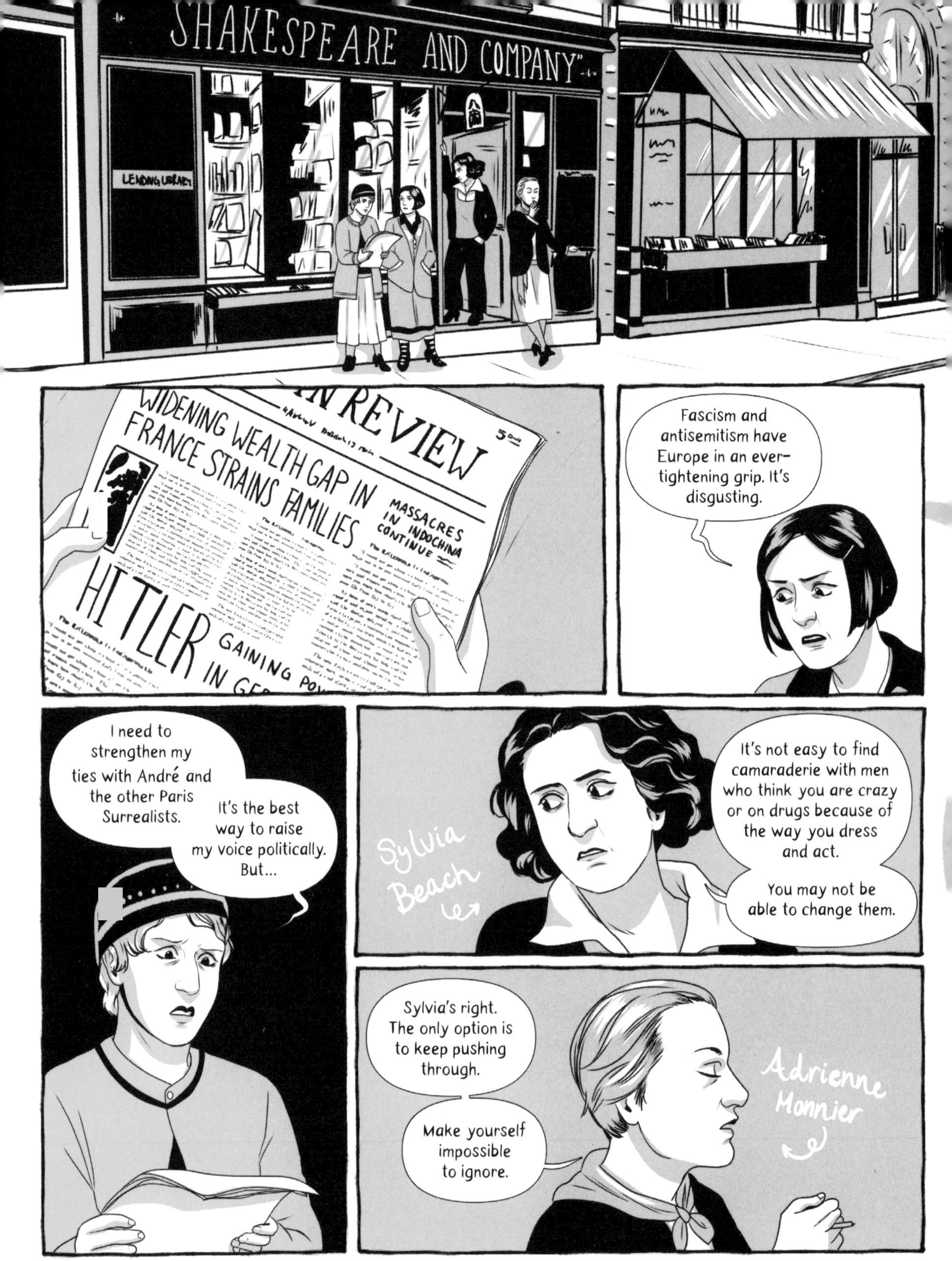

SHAKESPEARE AND COMPANY
LENDING LIBRARY
WIDENING WEALTH GAP IN FRANCE STRAINS FAMILIES
MASSACRES IN INDOCHINA CONTINUE
HITLER GAINING
Fascism and antisemitism have Europe in an ever-tightening grip. It's disgusting.
I need to strengthen my ties with André and the other Paris Surrealists.
It's the best way to raise my voice politically. But...
Sylvia Beach
It's not easy to find camaraderie with men who think you are crazy or on drugs because of the way you dress and act.
You may not be able to change them.
Sylvia's right. The only option is to keep pushing through.
Make yourself impossible to ignore.
Adrienne Monnier

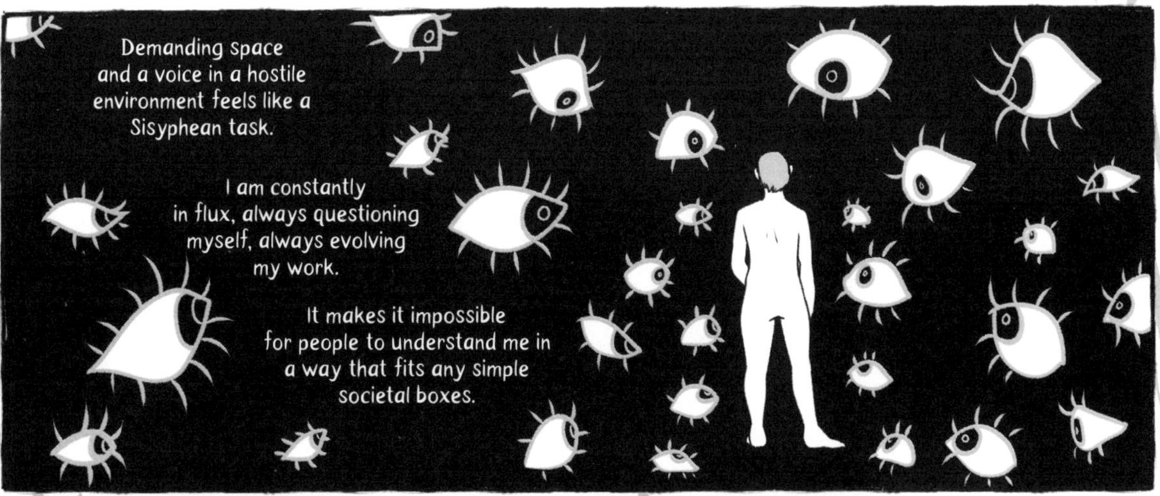
Demanding space and a voice in a hostile environment feels like a Sisyphean task.
I am constantly in flux, always questioning myself, always evolving my work.
It makes it impossible for people to understand me in a way that fits any simple societal boxes.

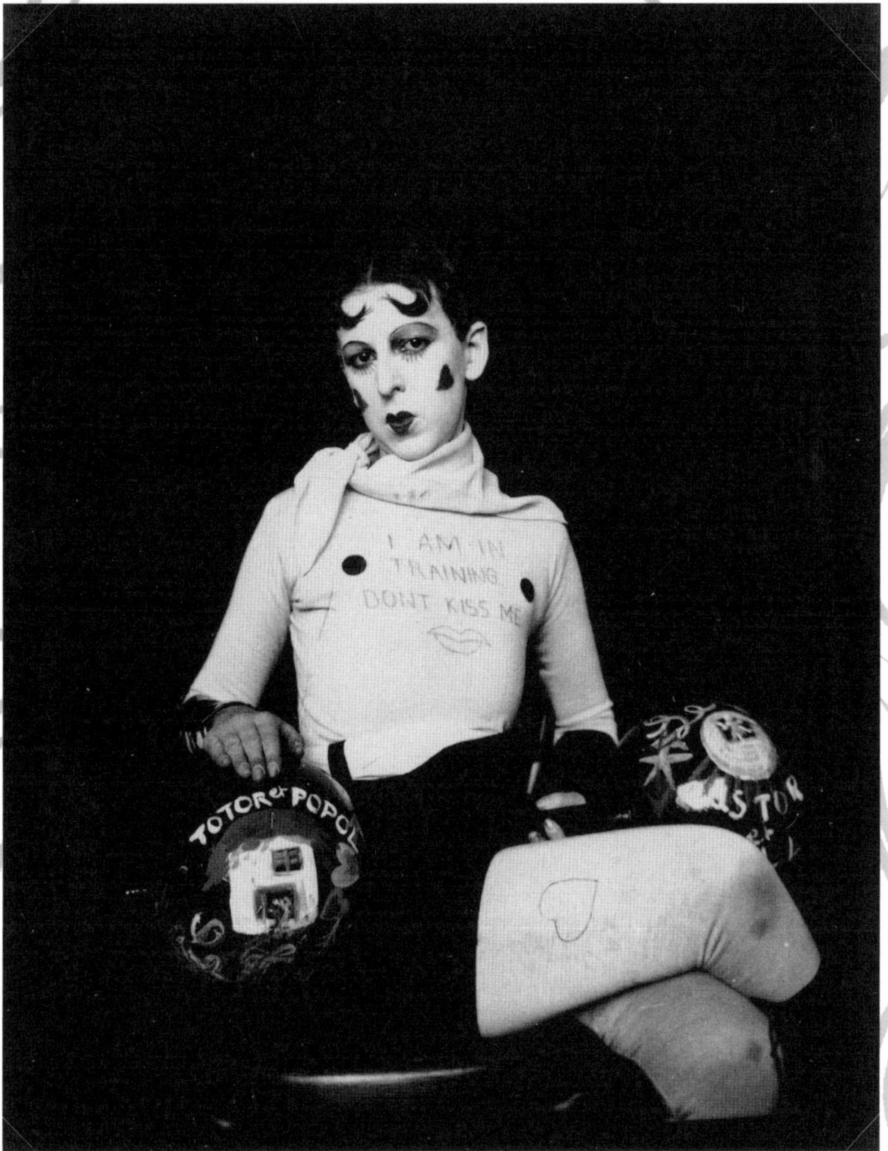
I AM IN TRAINING DONT KISS ME
TOTOR & POPOL

Good. That's the challenge I want people to face.

Are your boxes necessary to know me, to love me?

I didn't know the answer yet either.

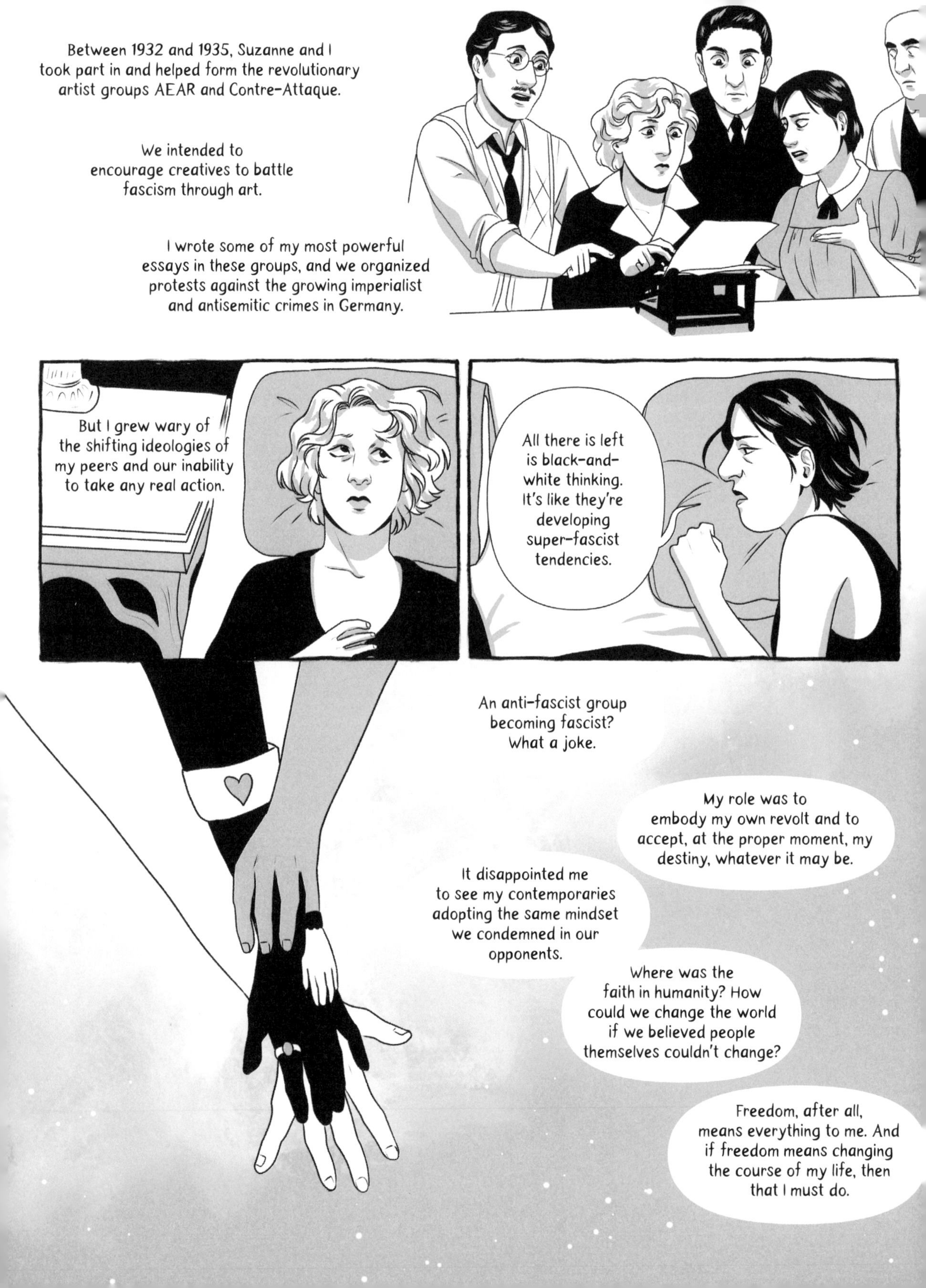
Between 1932 and 1935, Suzanne and I took part in and helped form the revolutionary artist groups AEAR and Contre-Attaque.
We intended to encourage creatives to battle fascism through art.
I wrote some of my most powerful essays in these groups, and we organized protests against the growing imperialist and antisemitic crimes in Germany.
But I grew wary of the shifting ideologies of my peers and our inability to take any real action.
All there is left is black-and-white thinking. It's like they're developing super-fascist tendencies.
An anti-fascist group becoming fascist? What a joke.
My role was to embody my own revolt and to accept, at the proper moment, my destiny, whatever it may be.
It disappointed me to see my contemporaries adopting the same mindset we condemned in our opponents.
Where was the faith in humanity? How could we change the world if we believed people themselves couldn't change?
Freedom, after all, means everything to me. And if freedom means changing the course of my life, then that I must do.

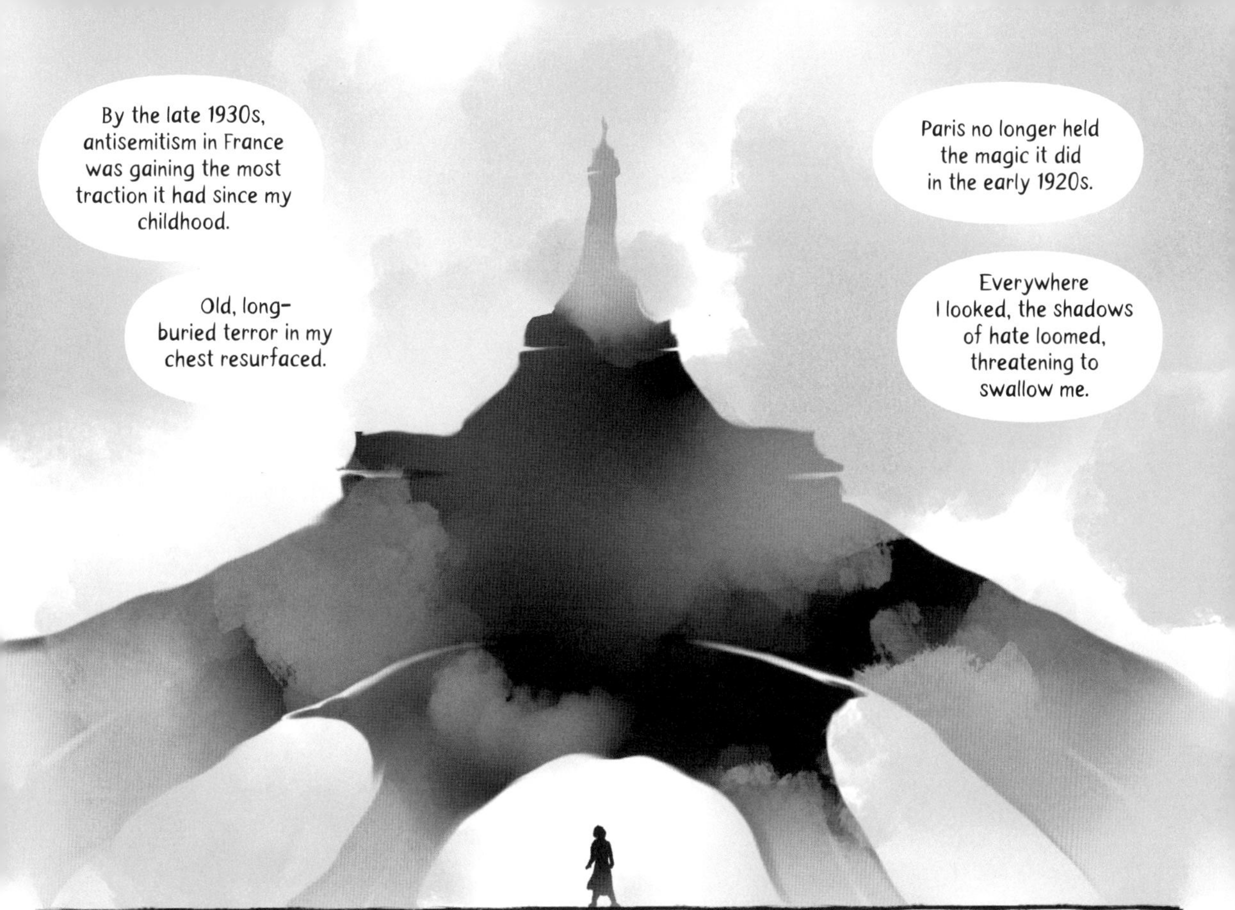
By the late 1930s, antisemitism in France was gaining the most traction it had since my childhood.
Old, long-buried terror in my chest resurfaced.
Paris no longer held the magic it did in the early 1920s.
Everywhere I looked, the shadows of hate loomed, threatening to swallow me.

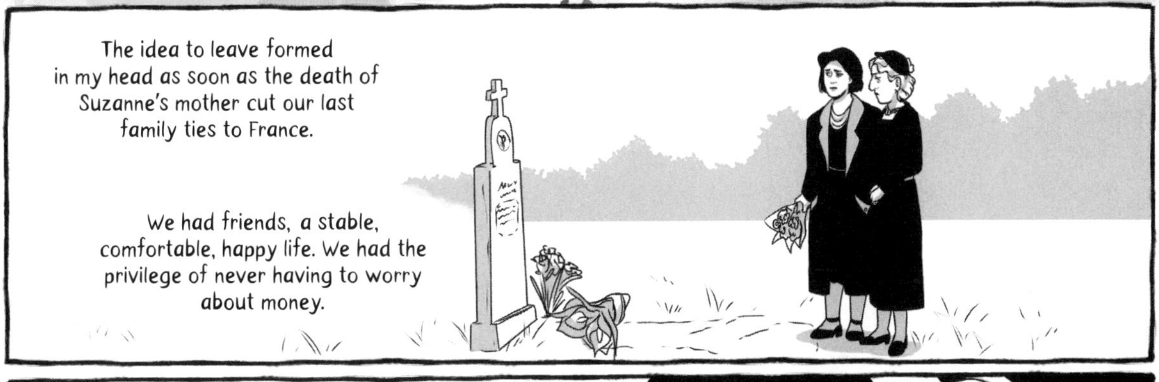
The idea to leave formed in my head as soon as the death of Suzanne's mother cut our last family ties to France.
We had friends, a stable, comfortable, happy life. We had the privilege of never having to worry about money.

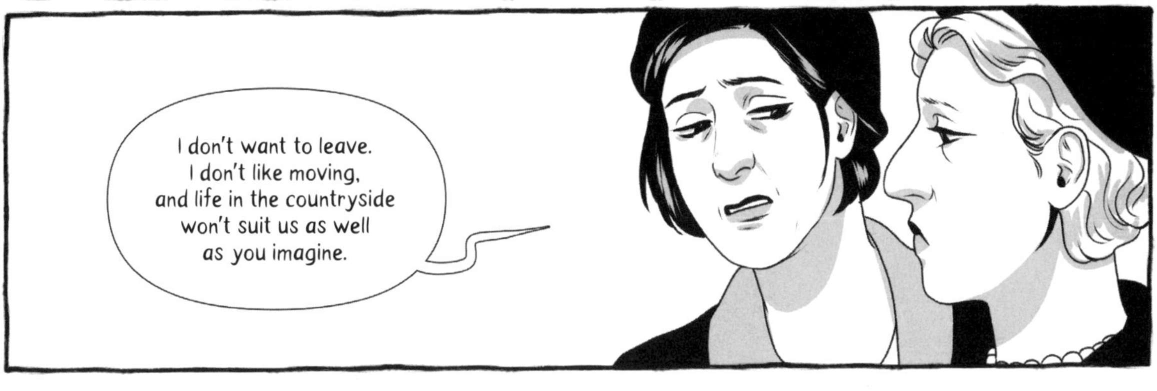
I don't want to leave. I don't like moving, and life in the countryside won't suit us as well as you imagine.

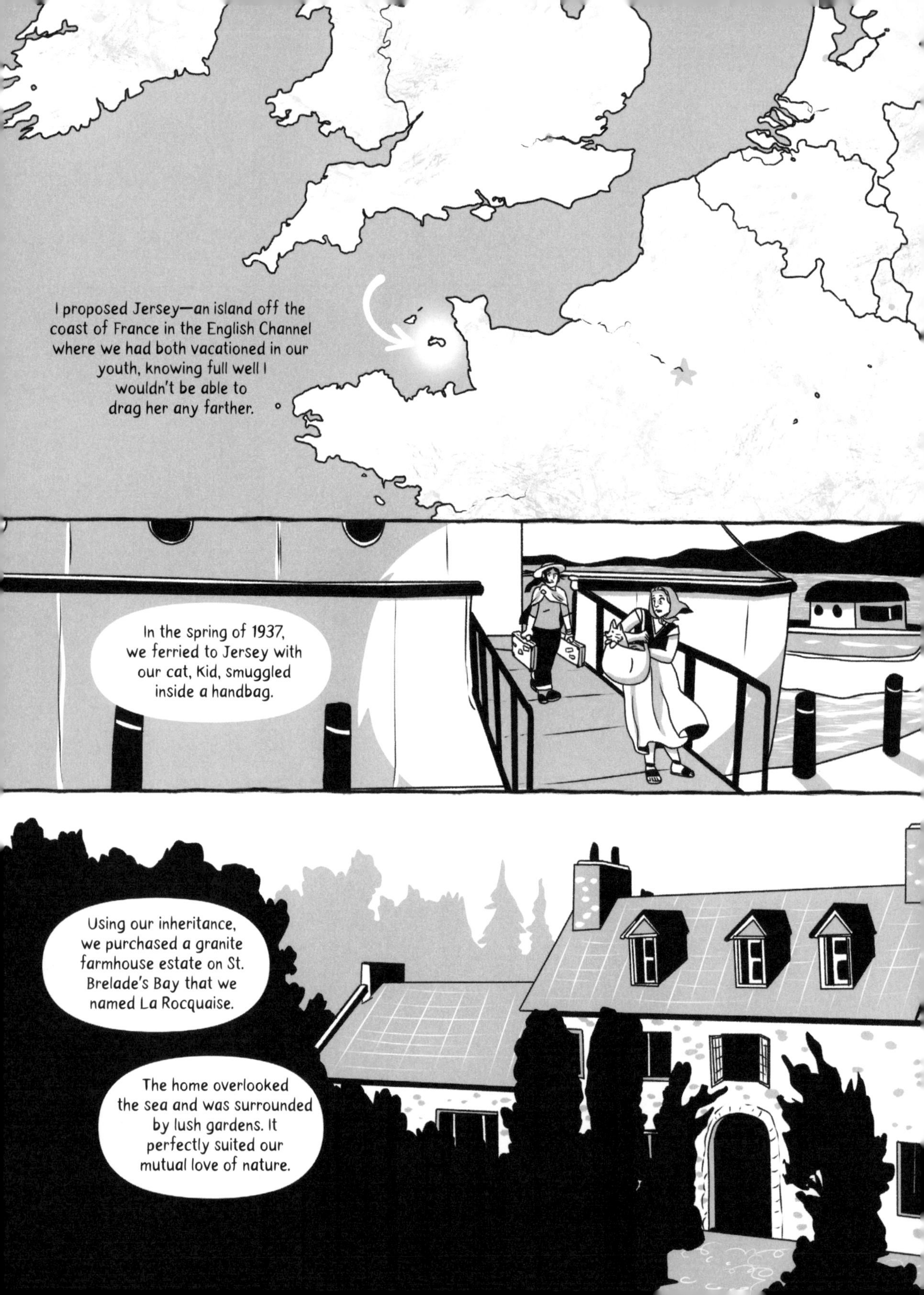
I proposed Jersey—an island off the coast of France in the English Channel where we had both vacationed in our youth, knowing full well I wouldn't be able to drag her any farther.
In the spring of 1937, we ferried to Jersey with our cat, Kid, smuggled inside a handbag.
Using our inheritance, we purchased a granite farmhouse estate on St. Brelade's Bay that we named La Rocquaise.
The home overlooked the sea and was surrounded by lush gardens. It perfectly suited our mutual love of nature.

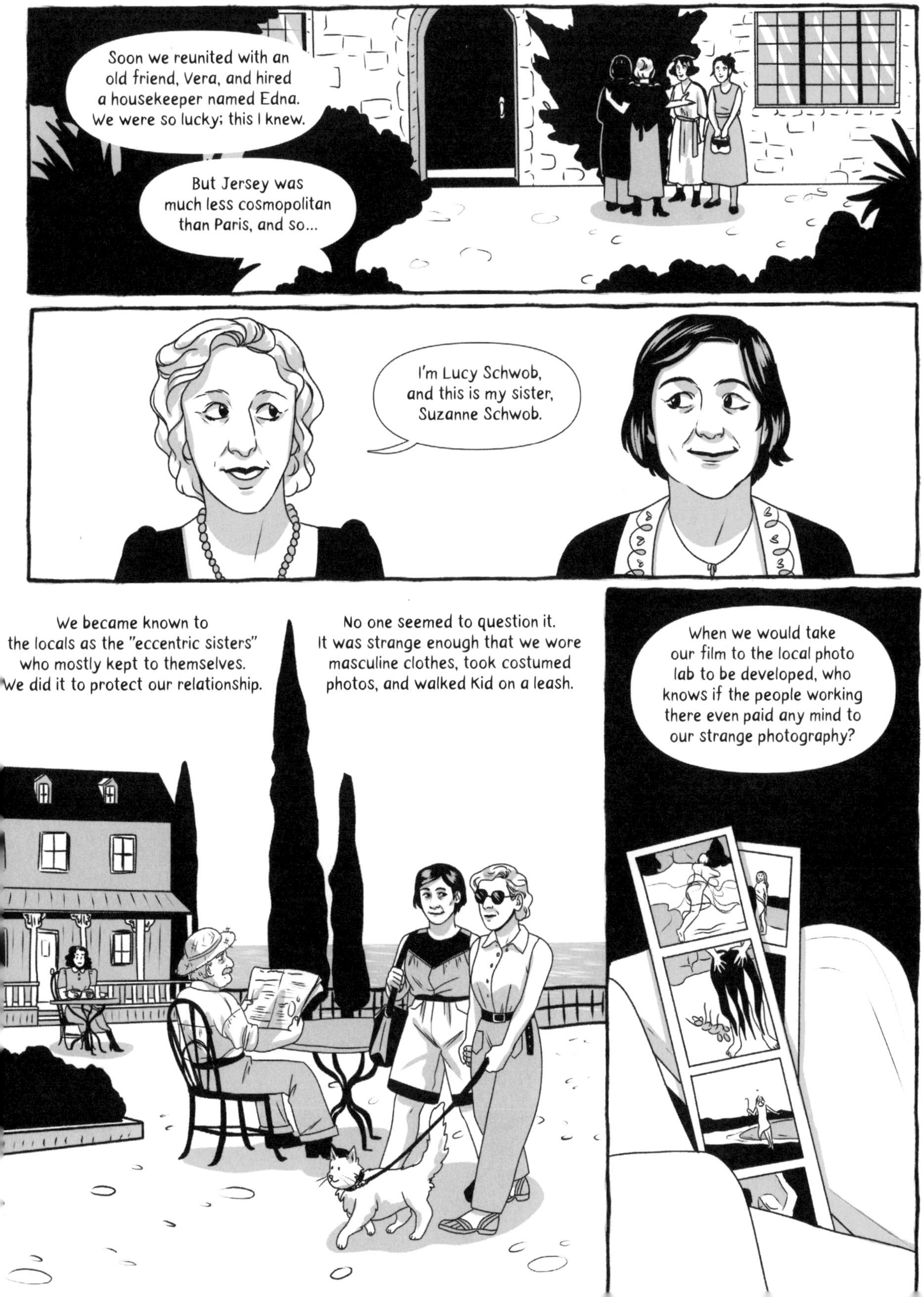

Soon we reunited with an old friend, Vera, and hired a housekeeper named Edna. We were so lucky; this I knew.
But Jersey was much less cosmopolitan than Paris, and so...
I'm Lucy Schwob, and this is my sister, Suzanne Schwob.
We became known to the locals as the "eccentric sisters" who mostly kept to themselves. We did it to protect our relationship.
No one seemed to question it. It was strange enough that we wore masculine clothes, took costumed photos, and walked Kid on a leash.
When we would take our film to the local photo lab to be developed, who knows if the people working there even paid any mind to our strange photography?

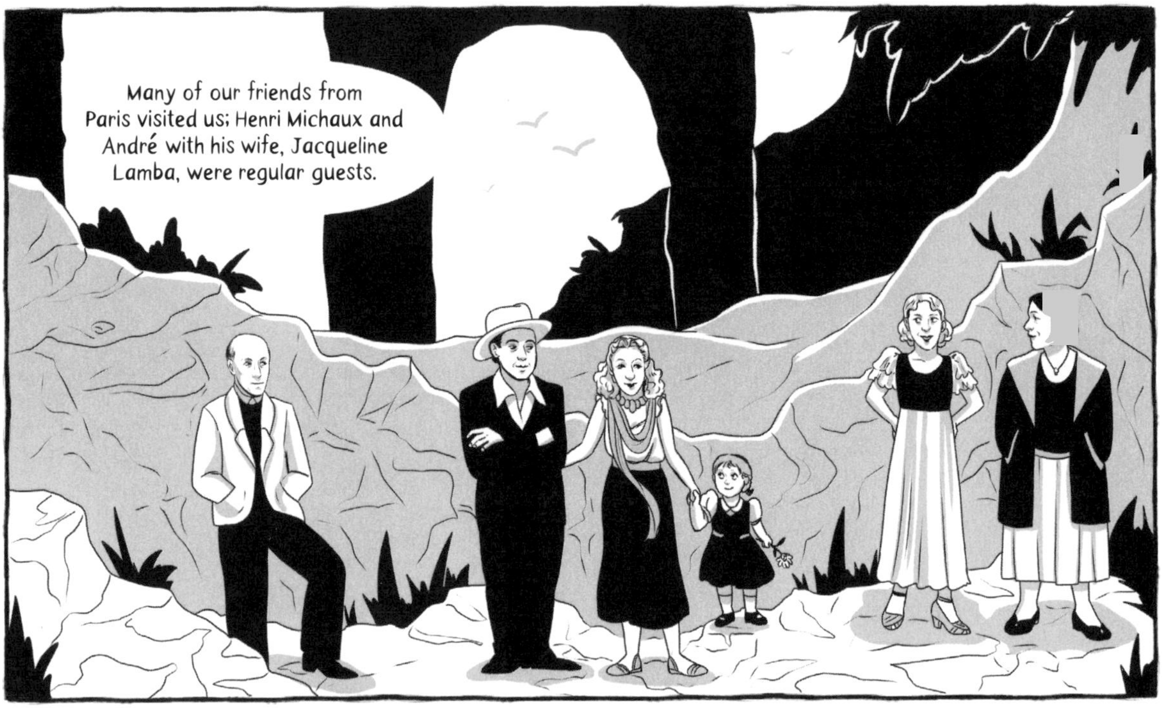
Many of our friends from Paris visited us; Henri Michaux and André with his wife, Jacqueline Lamba, were regular guests.

It was the illusion of a holiday without end.

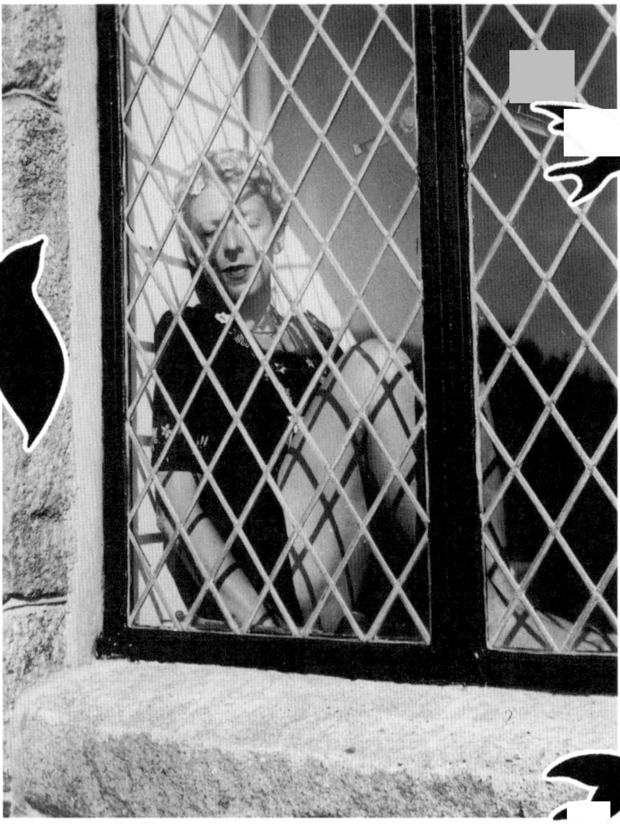

It seemed the only thing left to do was to become familiar with the trees, the birds, the doors, the windows and pulling from the clothing trunk the appropriate article, short or long, to dive into the sun and sea.

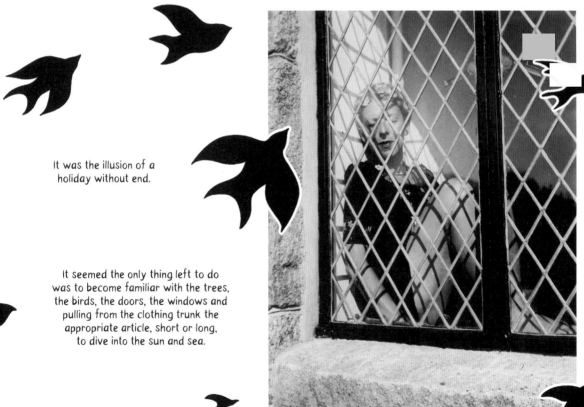

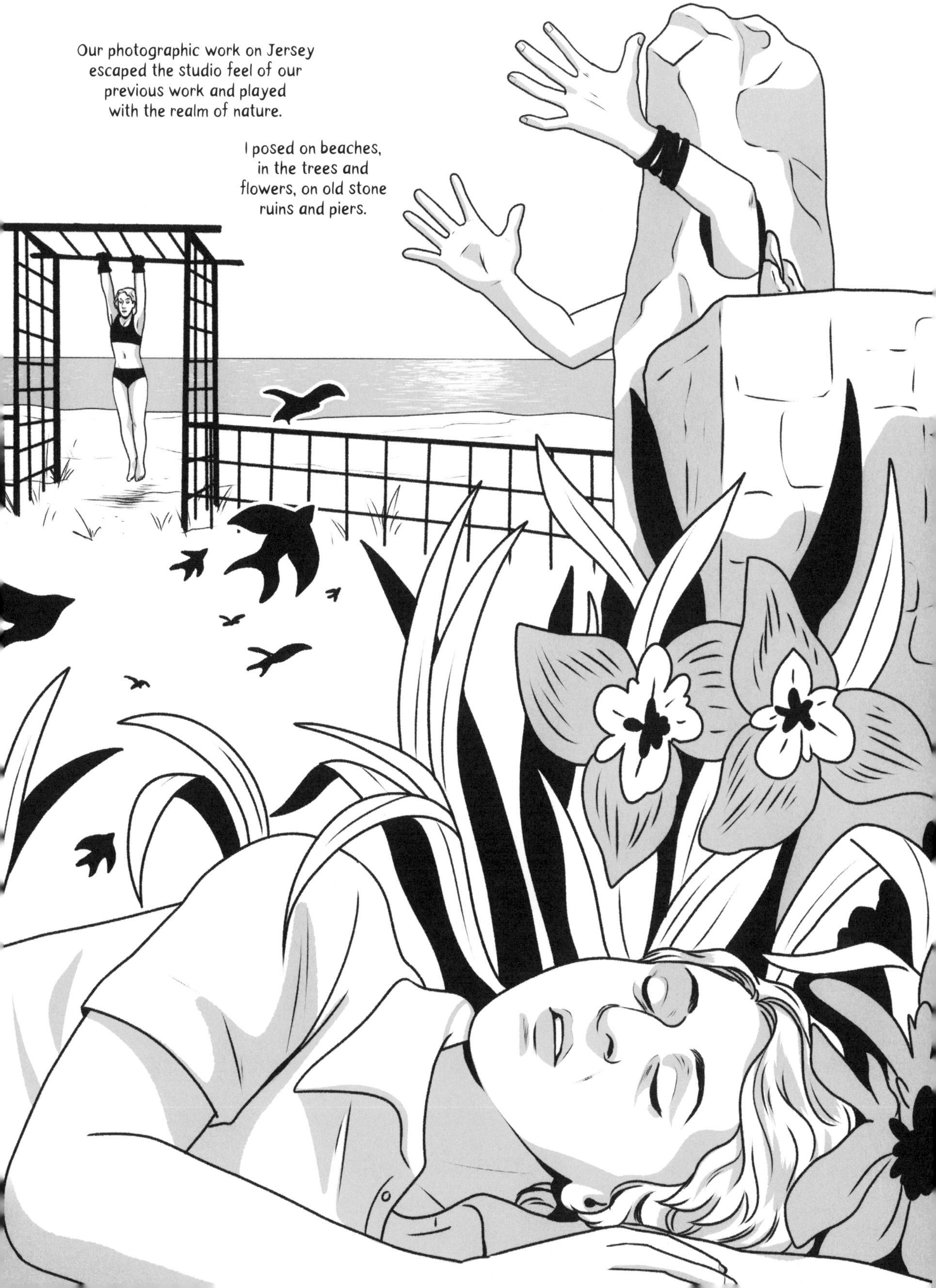
Our photographic work on Jersey escaped the studio feel of our previous work and played with the realm of nature.
I posed on beaches, in the trees and flowers, on old stone ruins and piers.

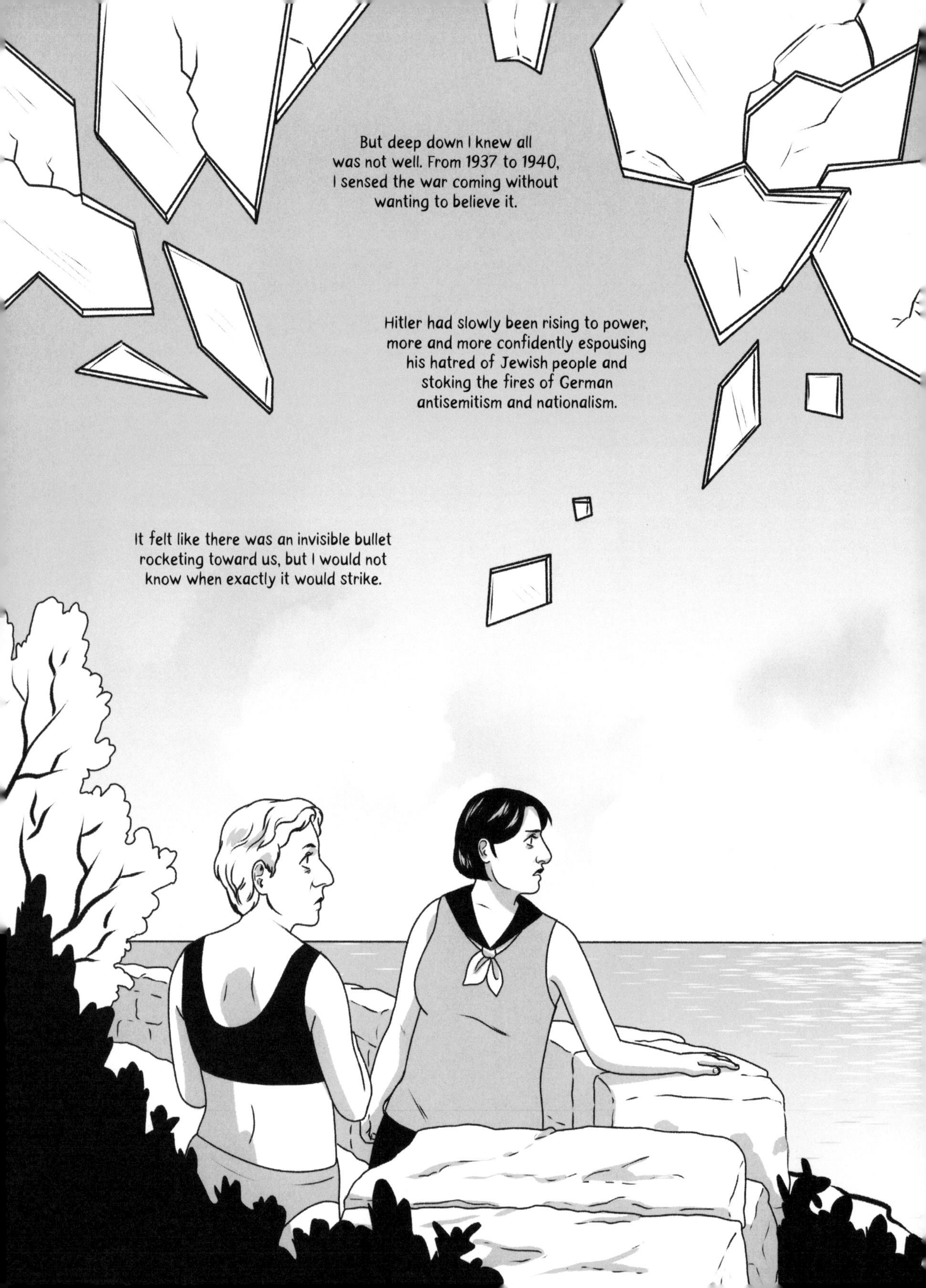
But deep down I knew all was not well. From 1937 to 1940, I sensed the war coming without wanting to believe it.
Hitler had slowly been rising to power, more and more confidently espousing his hatred of Jewish people and stoking the fires of German antisemitism and nationalism.
It felt like there was an invisible bullet rocketing toward us, but I would not know when exactly it would strike.

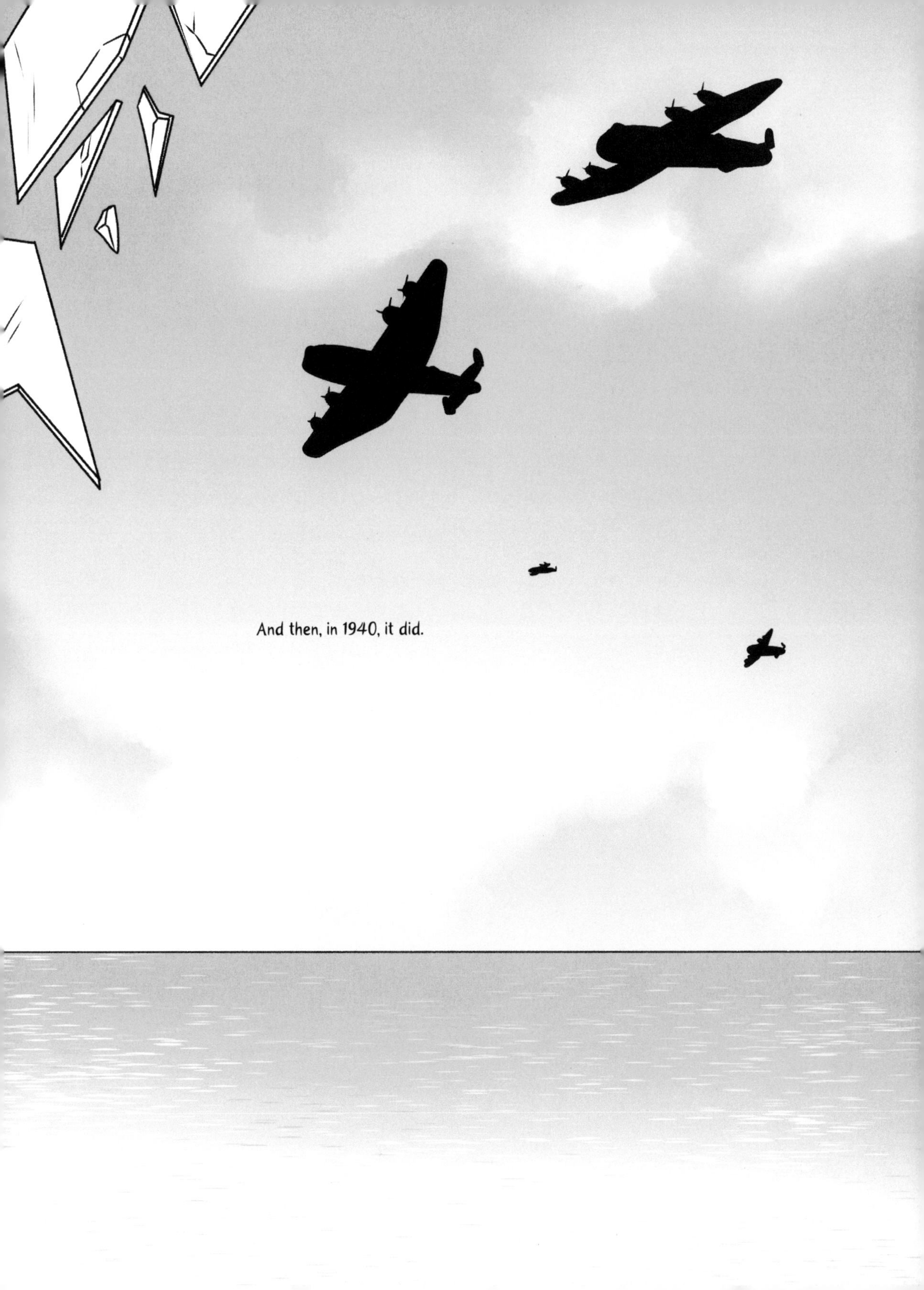
And then, in 1940, it did.

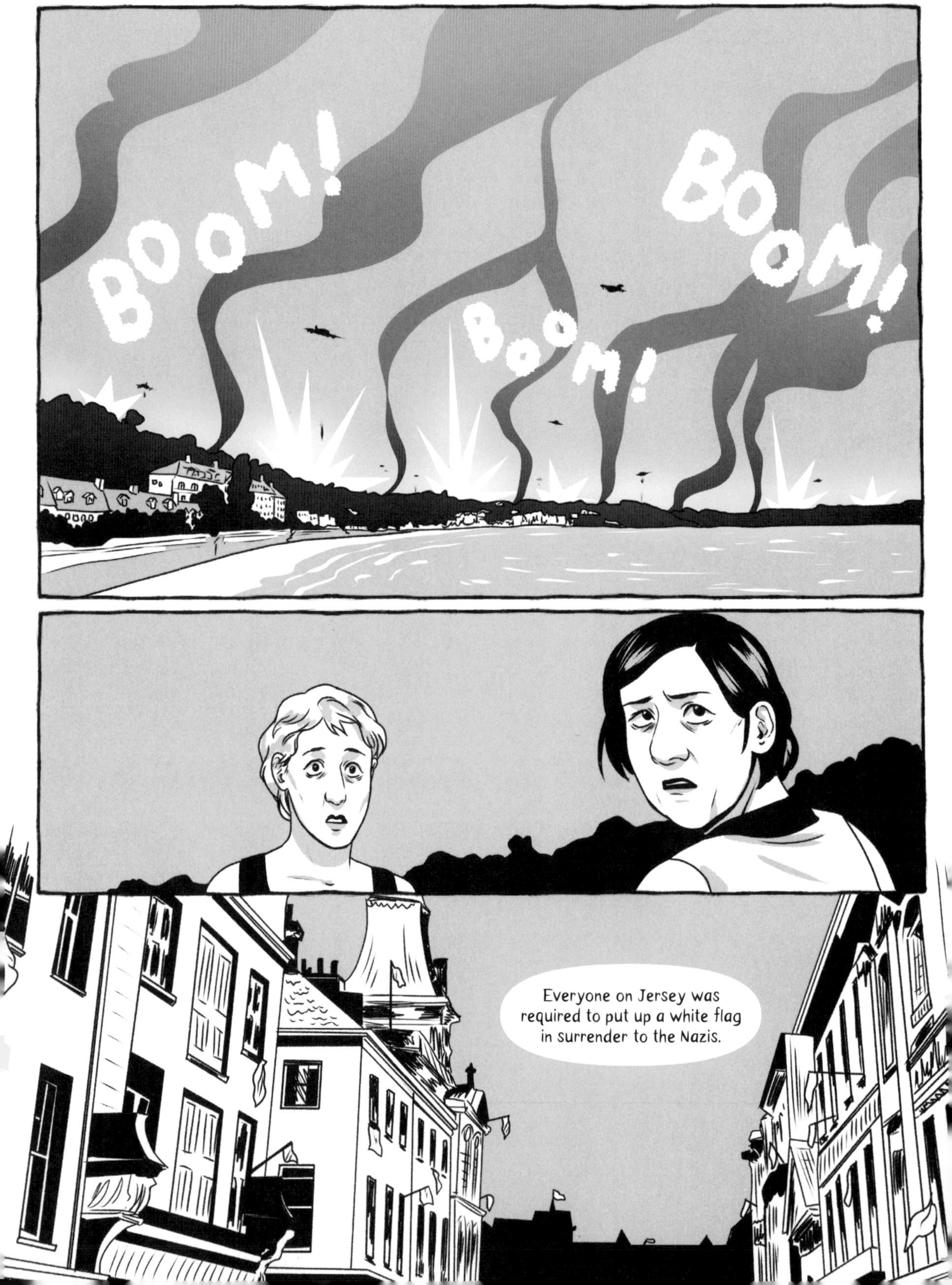
BOOM!
BOOM!
BOOM!
Everyone on Jersey was required to put up a white flag in surrender to the Nazis.

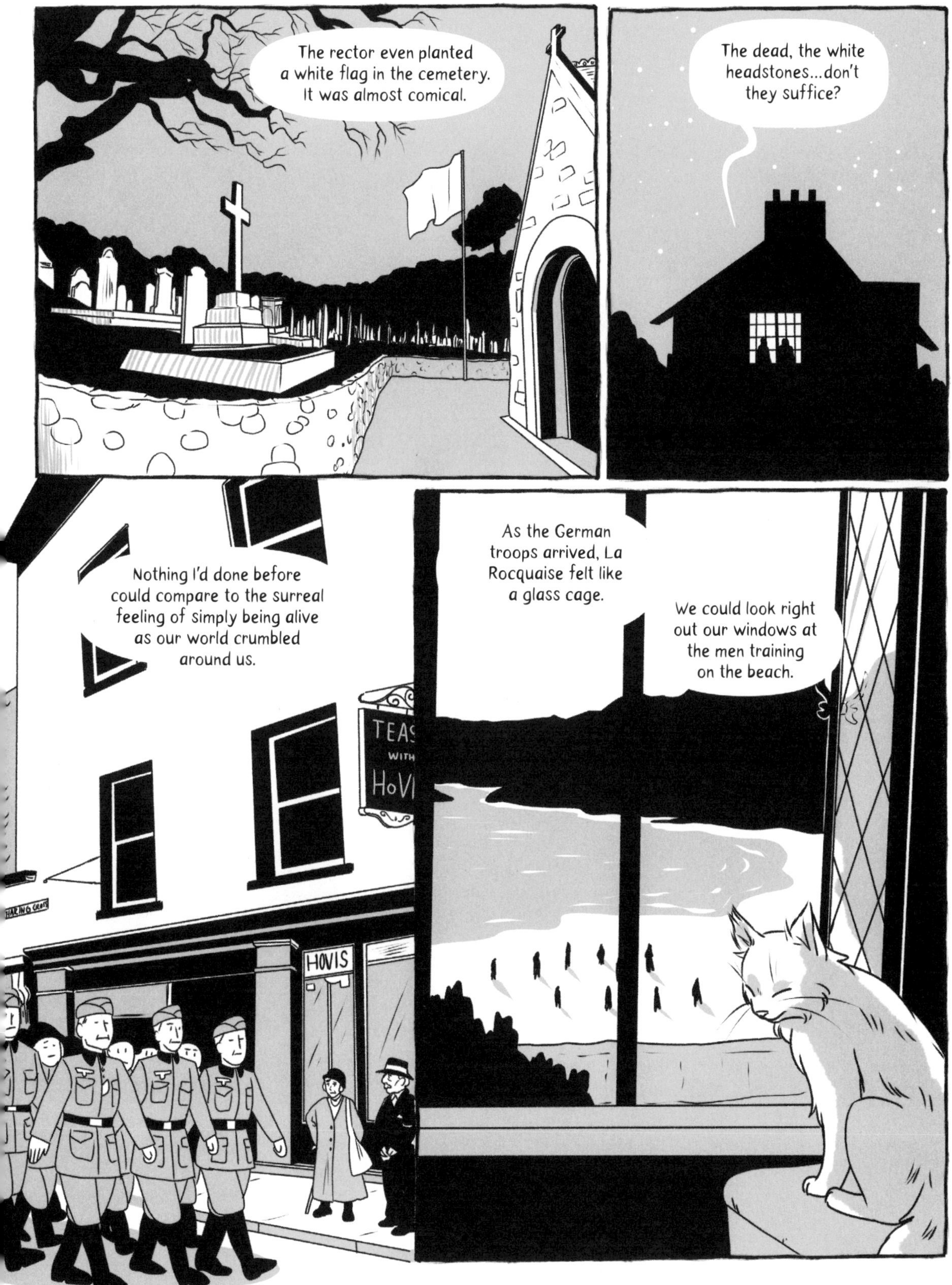

The rector even planted a white flag in the cemetery. It was almost comical.
The dead, the white headstones...don't they suffice?
Nothing I'd done before could compare to the surreal feeling of simply being alive as our world crumbled around us.
HOVIS
As the German troops arrived, La Rocquaise felt like a glass cage.
We could look right out our windows at the men training on the beach.

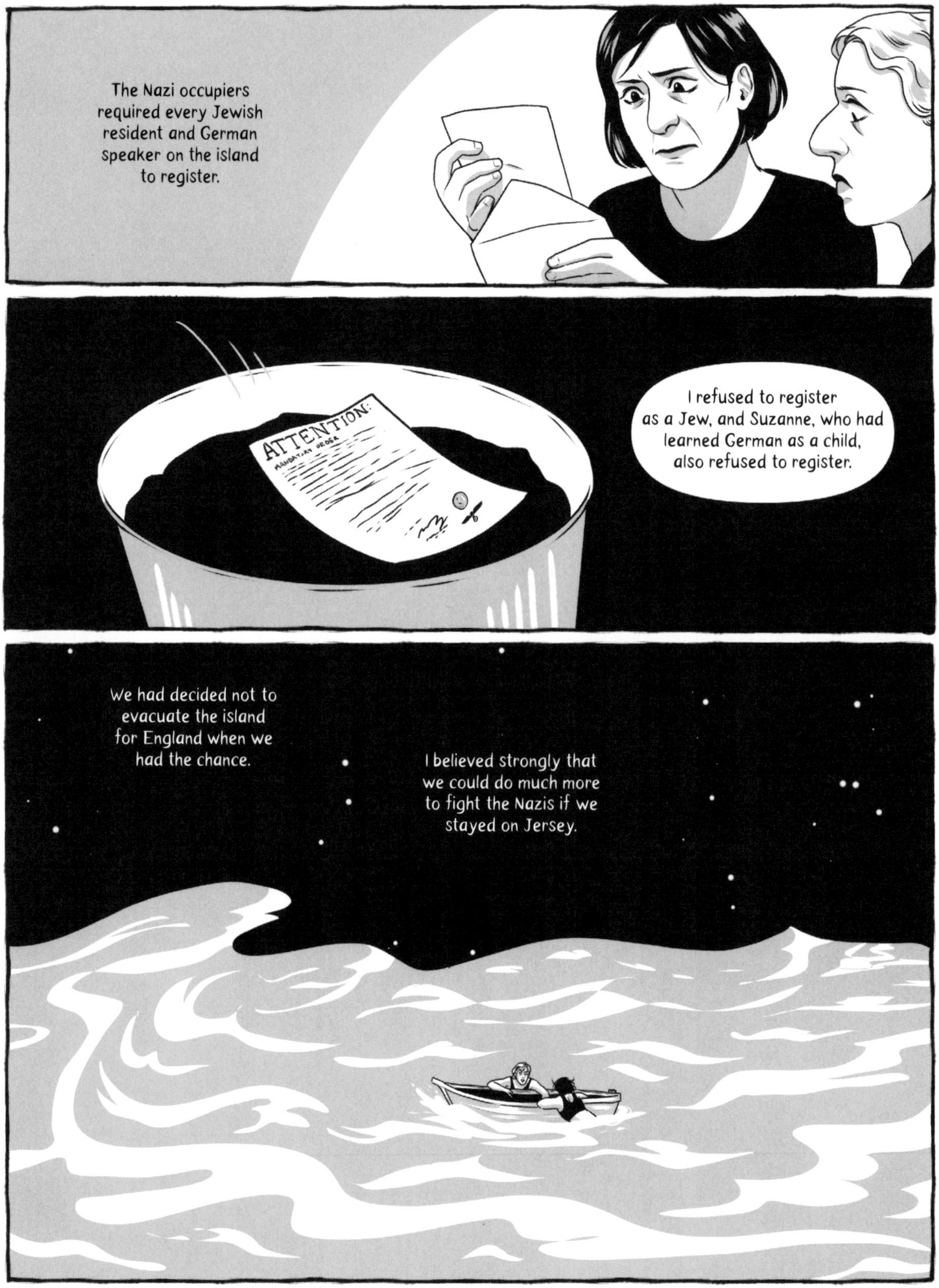
The Nazi occupiers required every Jewish resident and German speaker on the island to register.
ATTENTION:
MANDATORY ORDER
I refused to register as a Jew, and Suzanne, who had learned German as a child, also refused to register.
We had decided not to evacuate the island for England when we had the chance.
I believed strongly that we could do much more to fight the Nazis if we stayed on Jersey.

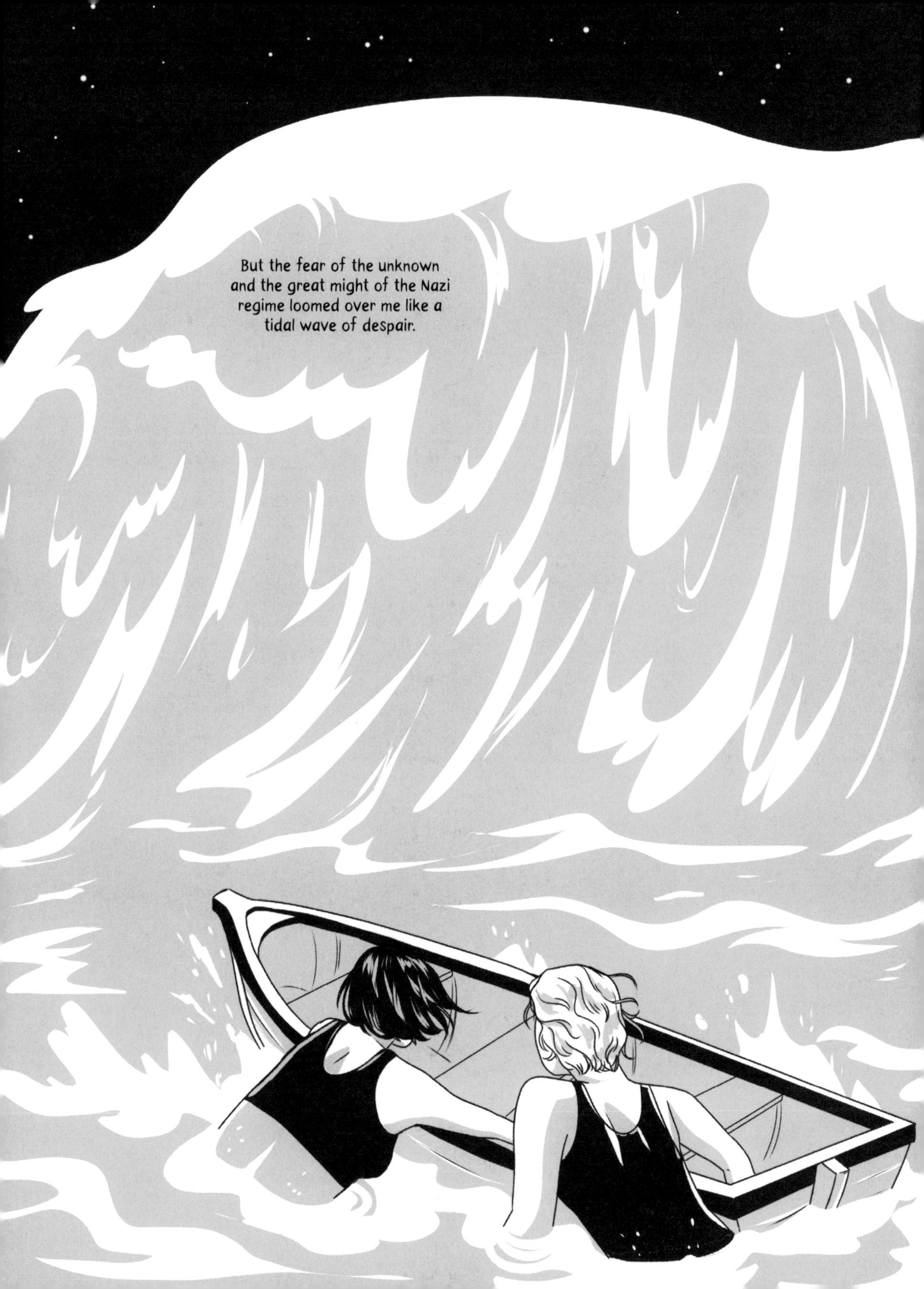
But the fear of the unknown and the great might of the Nazi regime loomed over me like a tidal wave of despair.

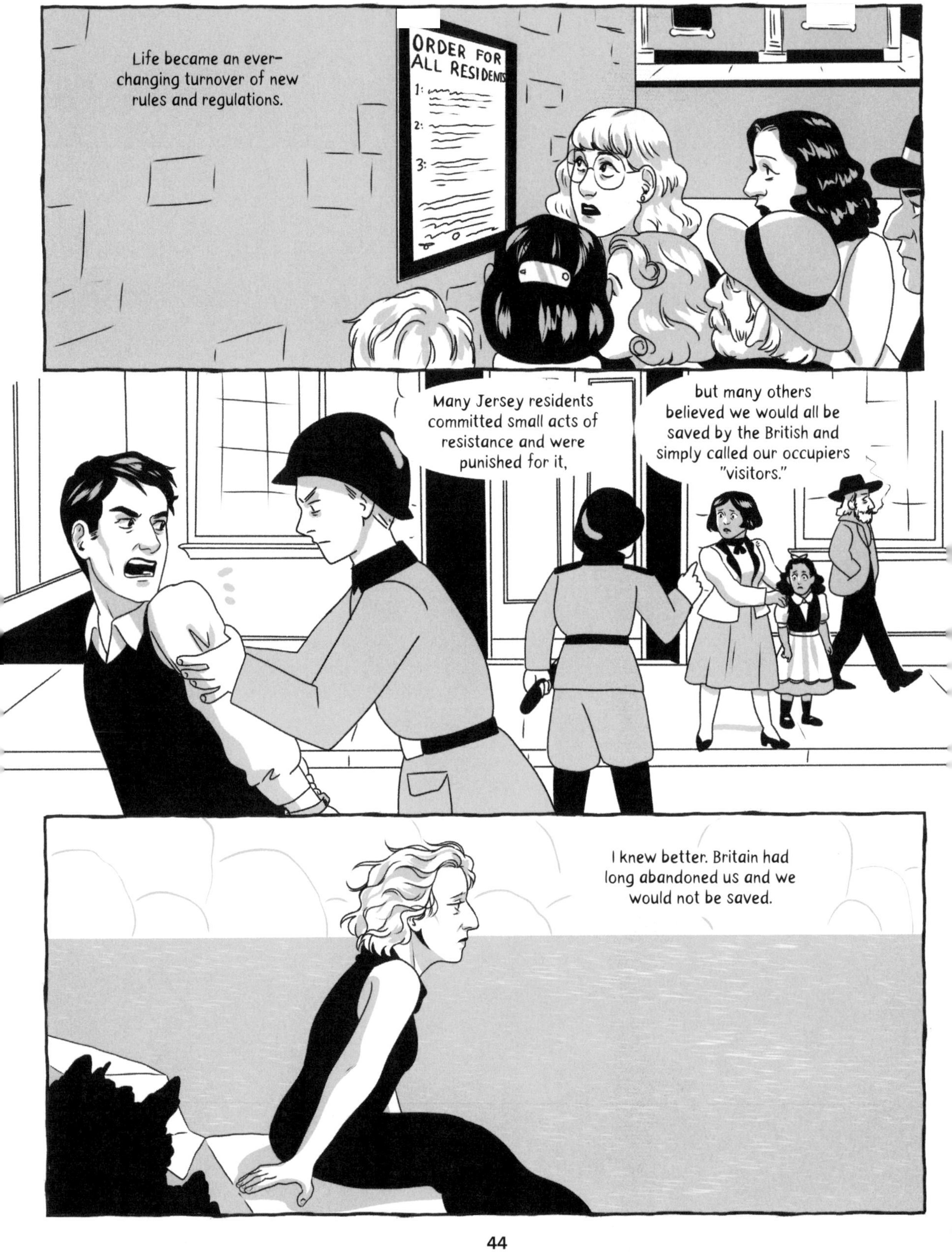
Life became an ever-changing turnover of new rules and regulations.
ORDER FOR ALL RESIDENTS
1:
2:
3:
Many Jersey residents committed small acts of resistance and were punished for it,
but many others believed we would all be saved by the British and simply called our occupiers "visitors."
I knew better. Britain had long abandoned us and we would not be saved.

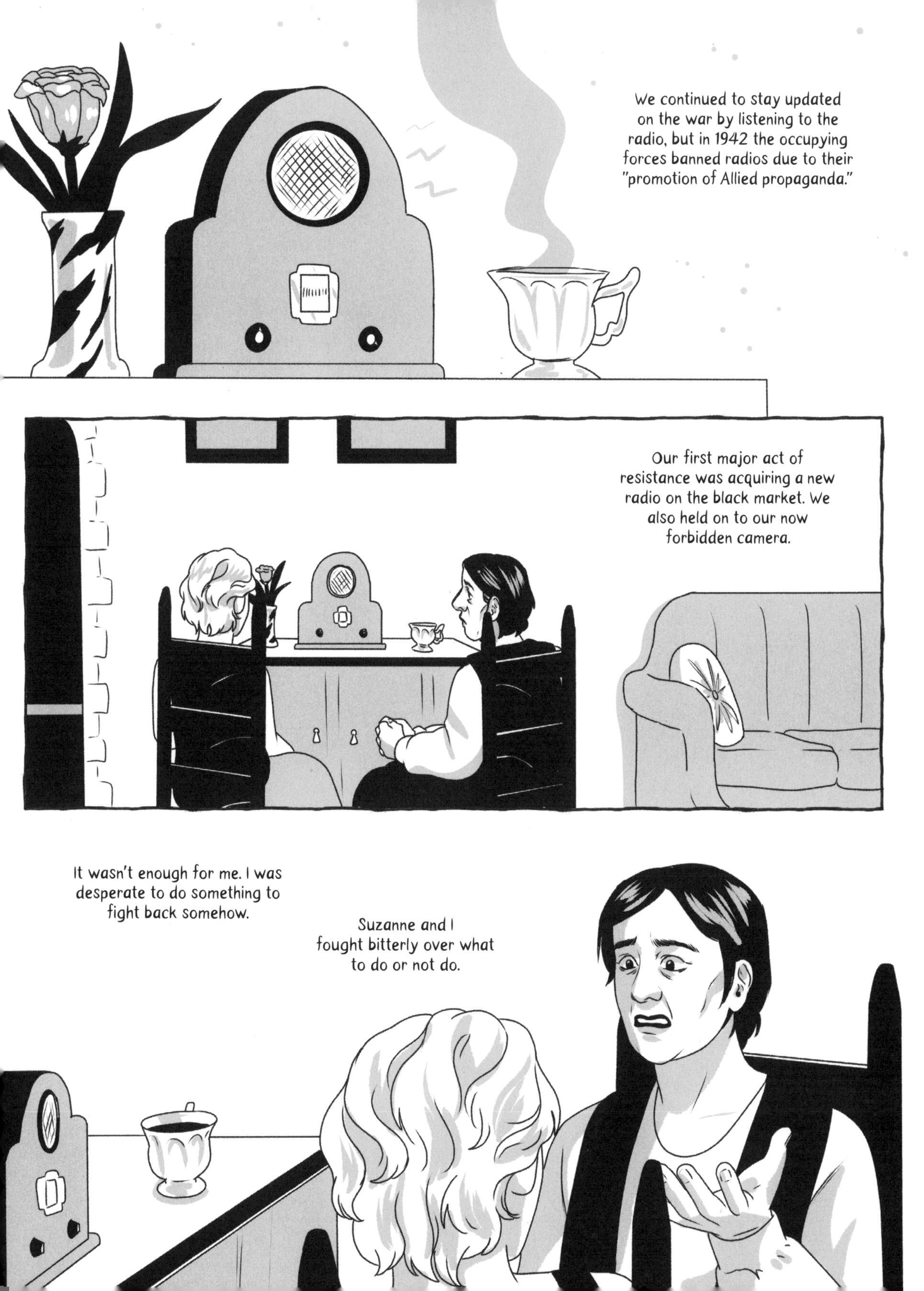
We continued to stay updated on the war by listening to the radio, but in 1942 the occupying forces banned radios due to their "promotion of Allied propaganda."
Our first major act of resistance was acquiring a new radio on the black market. We also held on to our now forbidden camera.
It wasn't enough for me. I was desperate to do something to fight back somehow.
Suzanne and I fought bitterly over what to do or not do.

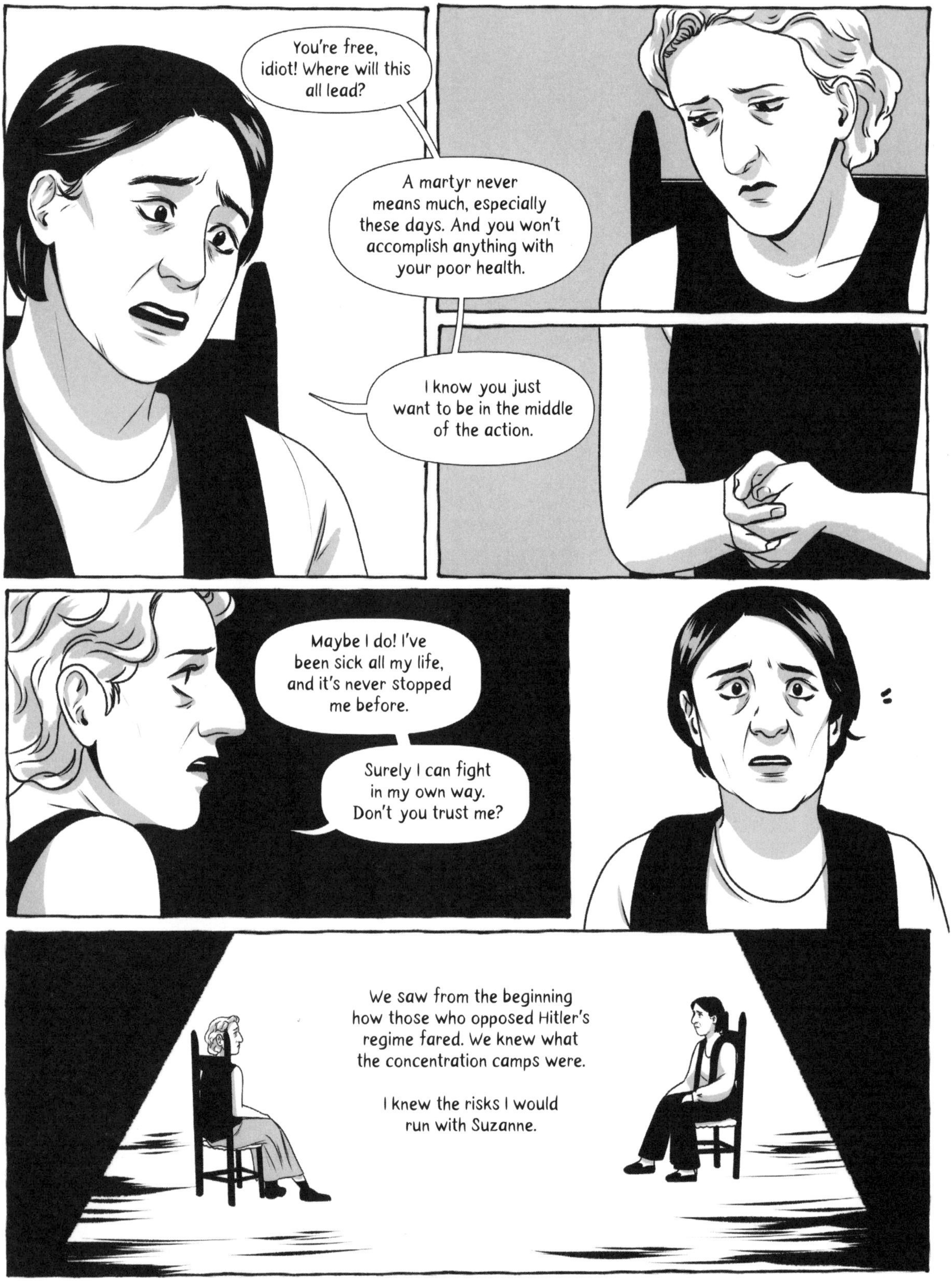
You're free, idiot! Where will this all lead?
A martyr never means much, especially these days. And you won't accomplish anything with your poor health.
I know you just want to be in the middle of the action.
Maybe I do! I've been sick all my life, and it's never stopped me before.
Surely I can fight in my own way. Don't you trust me?
We saw from the beginning how those who opposed Hitler's regime fared. We knew what the concentration camps were.
I knew the risks I would run with Suzanne.

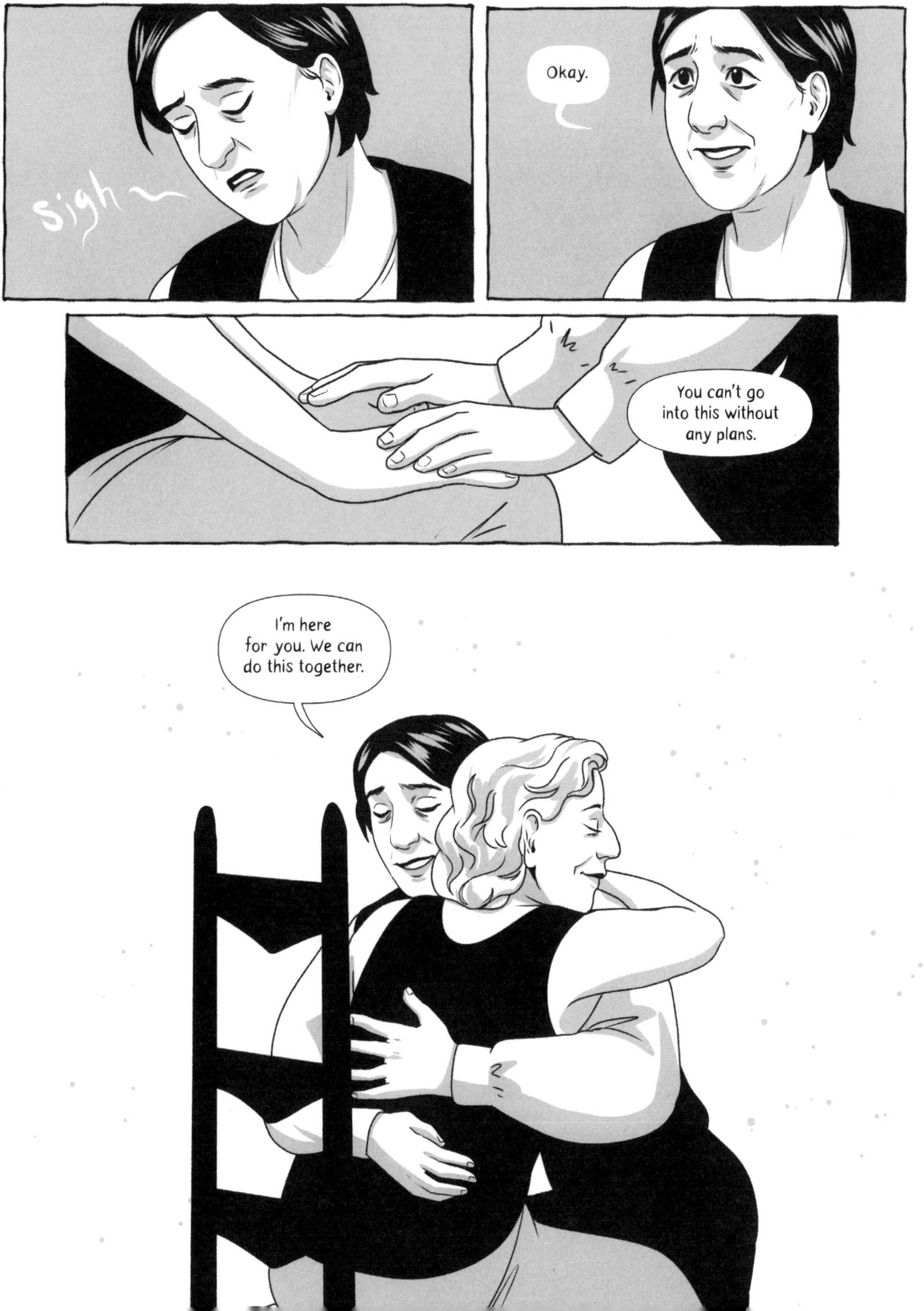
sigh
Okay.
You can't go into this without any plans.
I'm here for you. We can do this together.

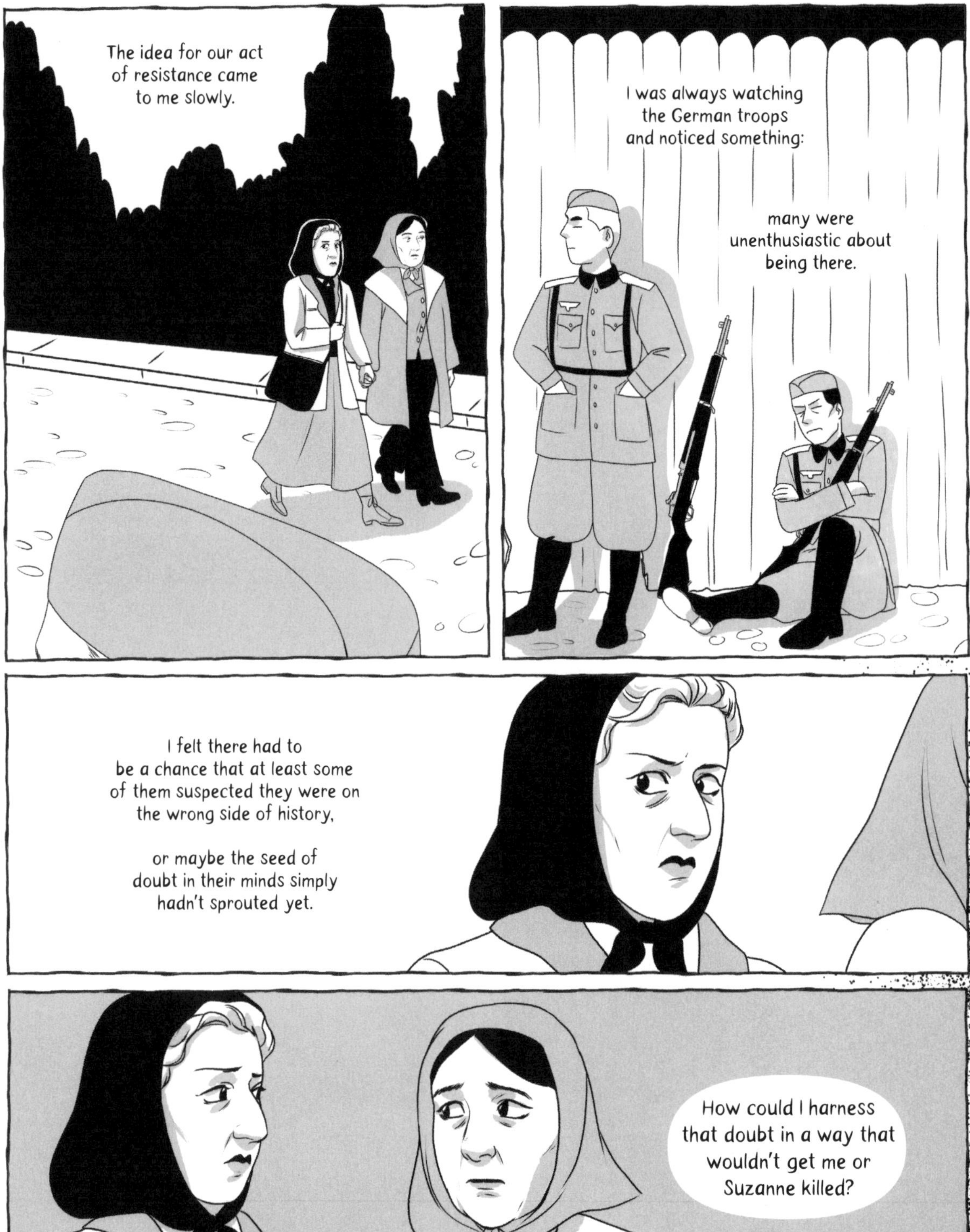
The idea for our act of resistance came to me slowly.
I was always watching the German troops and noticed something:
many were unenthusiastic about being there.
I felt there had to be a chance that at least some of them suspected they were on the wrong side of history,
or maybe the seed of doubt in their minds simply hadn't sprouted yet.
How could I harness that doubt in a way that wouldn't get me or Suzanne killed?

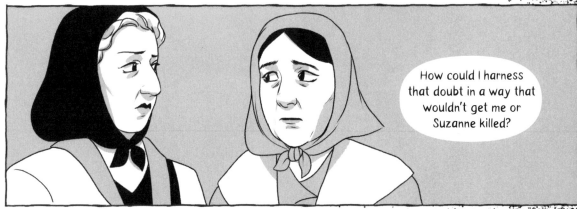

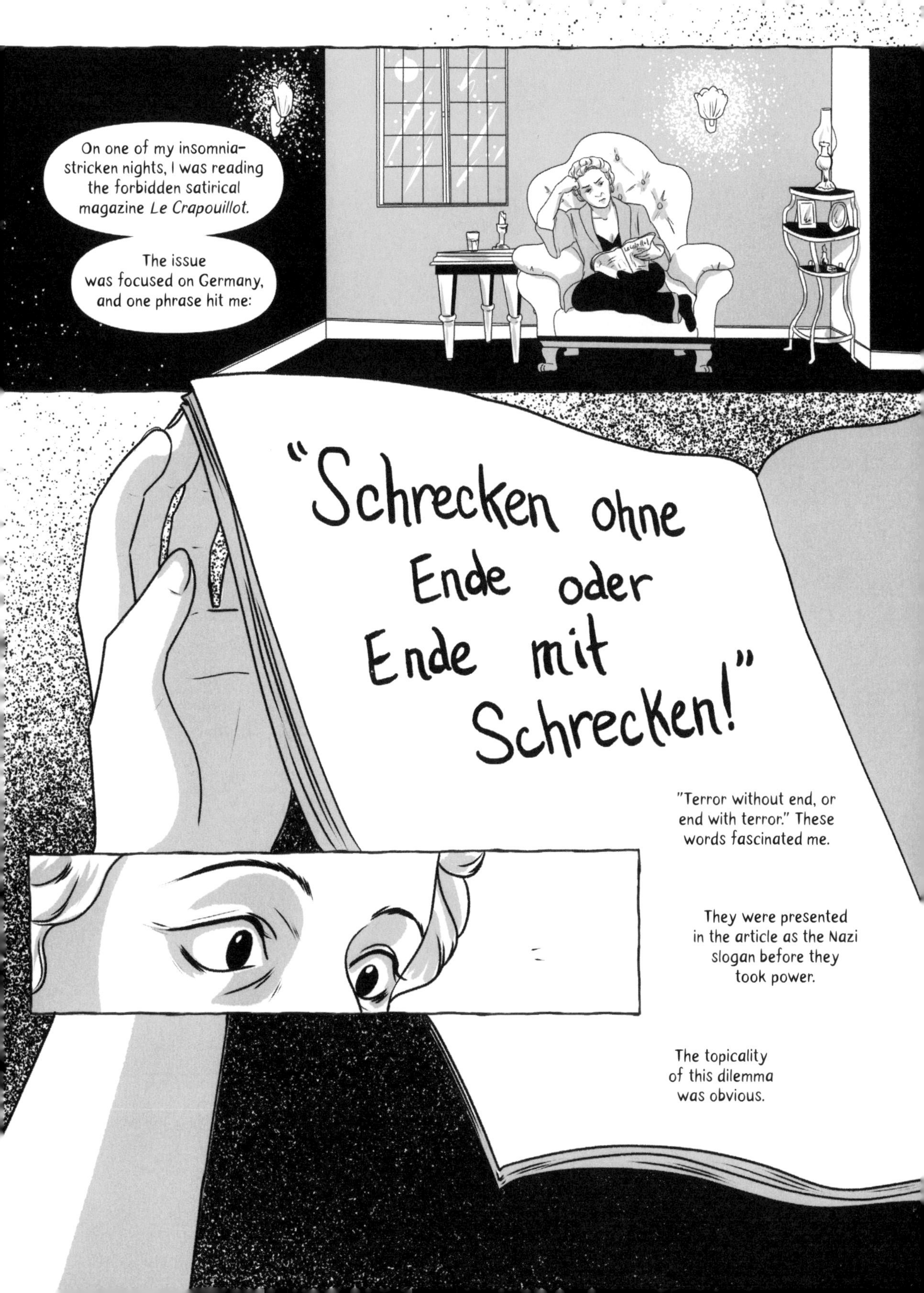
On one of my insomnia-stricken nights, I was reading the forbidden satirical magazine *Le Crapouillot.*
The issue was focused on Germany, and one phrase hit me:
"Schrecken ohne Ende oder Ende mit Schrecken!"
"Terror without end, or end with terror." These words fascinated me.
They were presented in the article as the Nazi slogan before they took power.
The topicality of this dilemma was obvious.

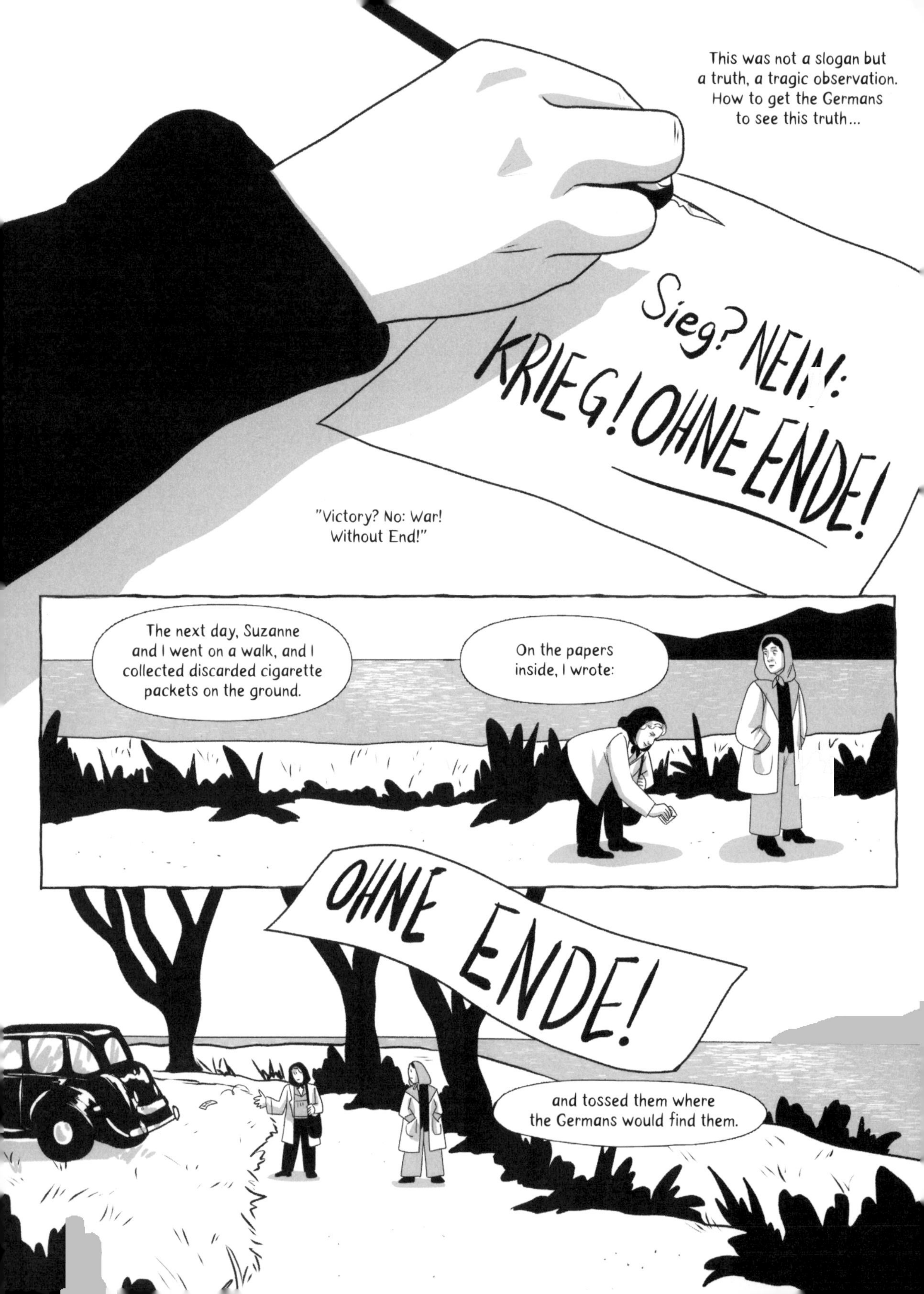
This was not a slogan but a truth, a tragic observation. How to get the Germans to see this truth...
Sieg? NEIN: KRIEG! OHNE ENDE!
"Victory? No: War! Without End!"
The next day, Suzanne and I went on a walk, and I collected discarded cigarette packets on the ground.
On the papers inside, I wrote:
OHNE ENDE!
and tossed them where the Germans would find them.

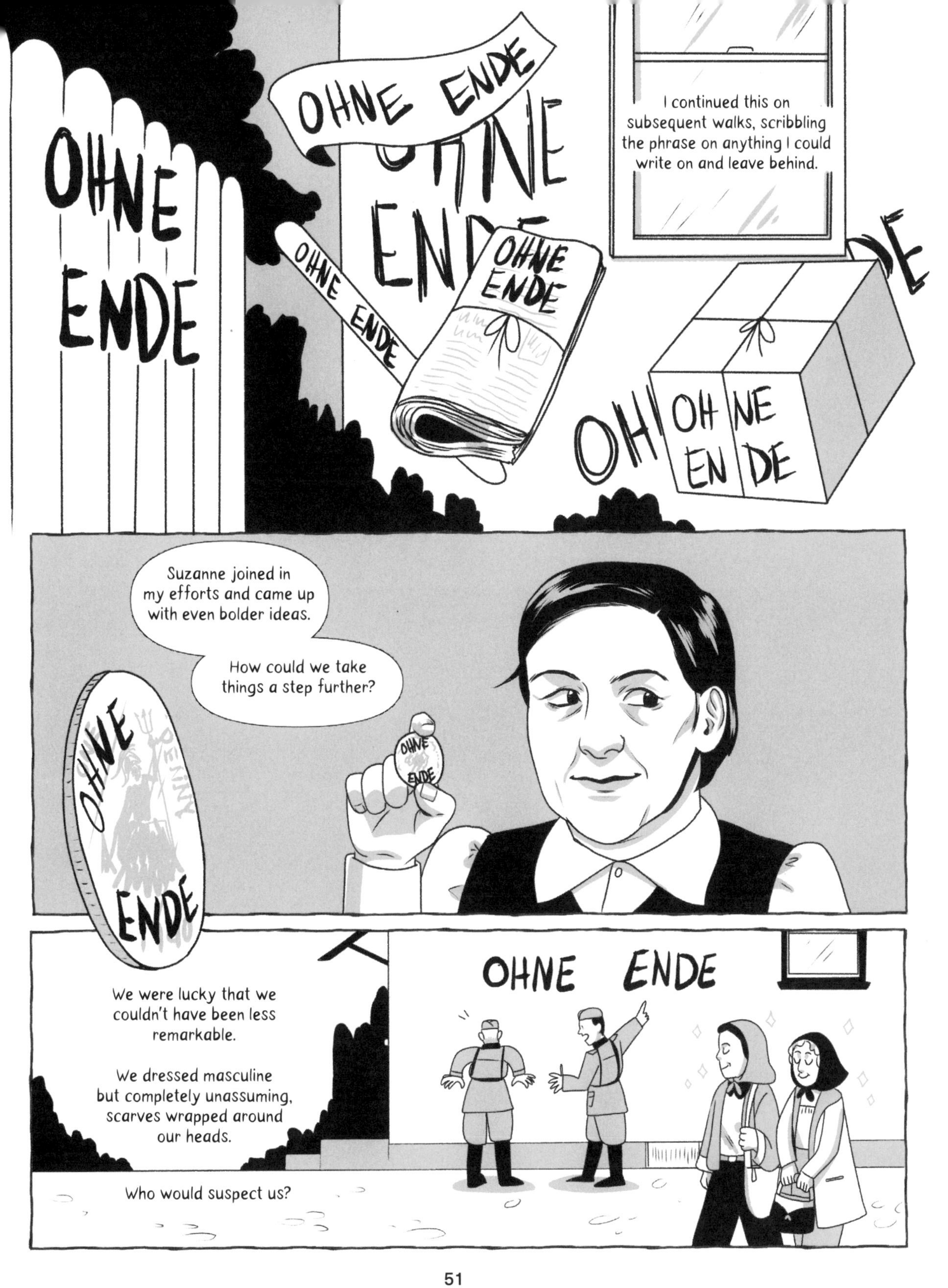
OHNE ENDE
OHNE ENDE
OHNE ENDE
I continued this on subsequent walks, scribbling the phrase on anything I could write on and leave behind.
OHNE ENDE
OHNE ENDE
OHNE ENDE
Suzanne joined in my efforts and came up with even bolder ideas.
How could we take things a step further?
OHNE ENDE
PENNY
We were lucky that we couldn't have been less remarkable.
We dressed masculine but completely unassuming, scarves wrapped around our heads.
Who would suspect us?
OHNE ENDE

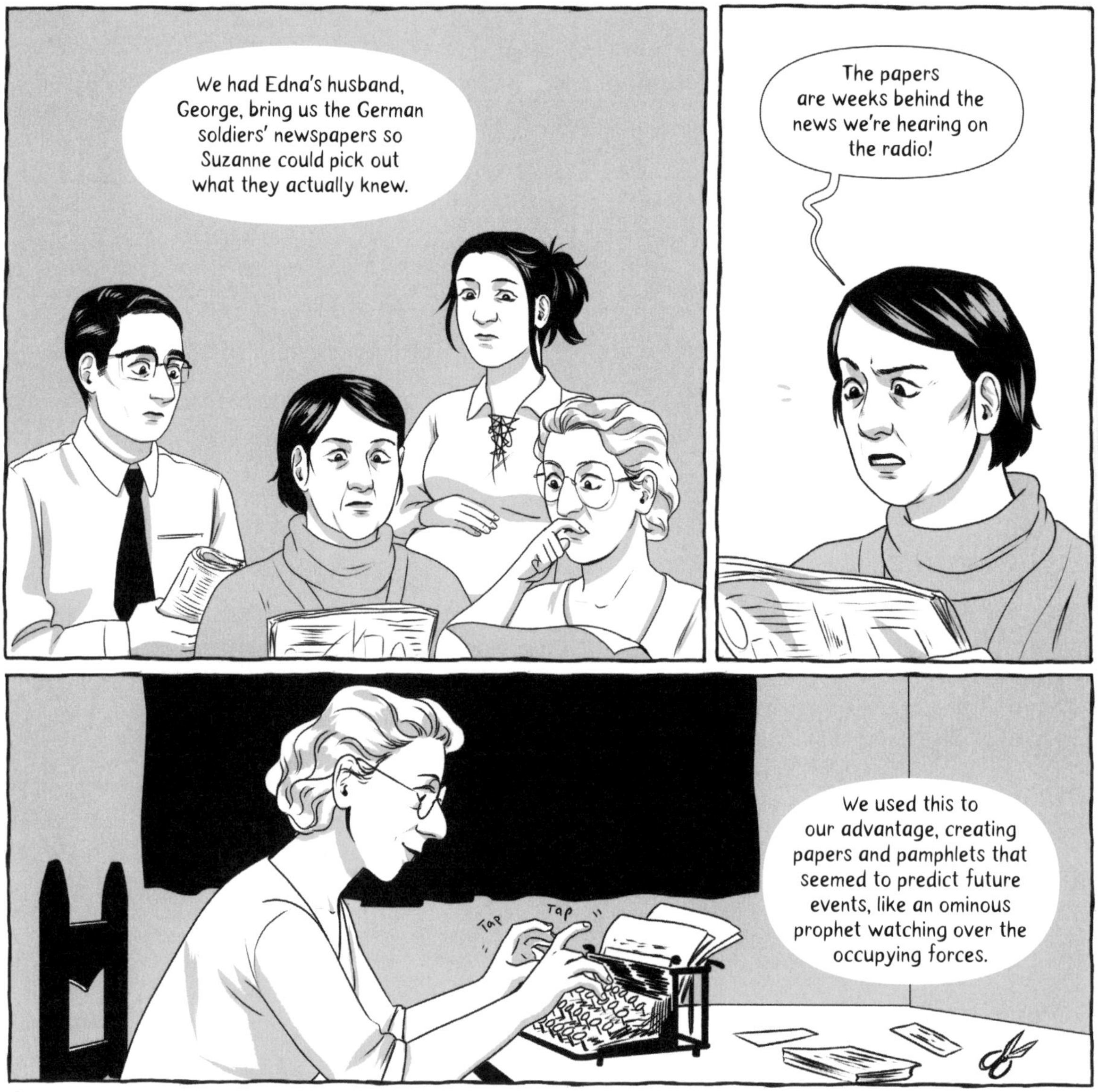
We had Edna's husband, George, bring us the German soldiers' newspapers so Suzanne could pick out what they actually knew.
The papers are weeks behind the news we're hearing on the radio!
Tap
Tap
We used this to our advantage, creating papers and pamphlets that seemed to predict future events, like an ominous prophet watching over the occupying forces.

We signed our tracts as "The Soldier with No Name."

Der Soldat ohne Namen

As if we, as this character, were one of the soldiers in their ranks, secretly speaking out to them on their own level.

A voice the same as theirs, who could understand their hardships and their homesickness. We could weaponize their spirits from within.

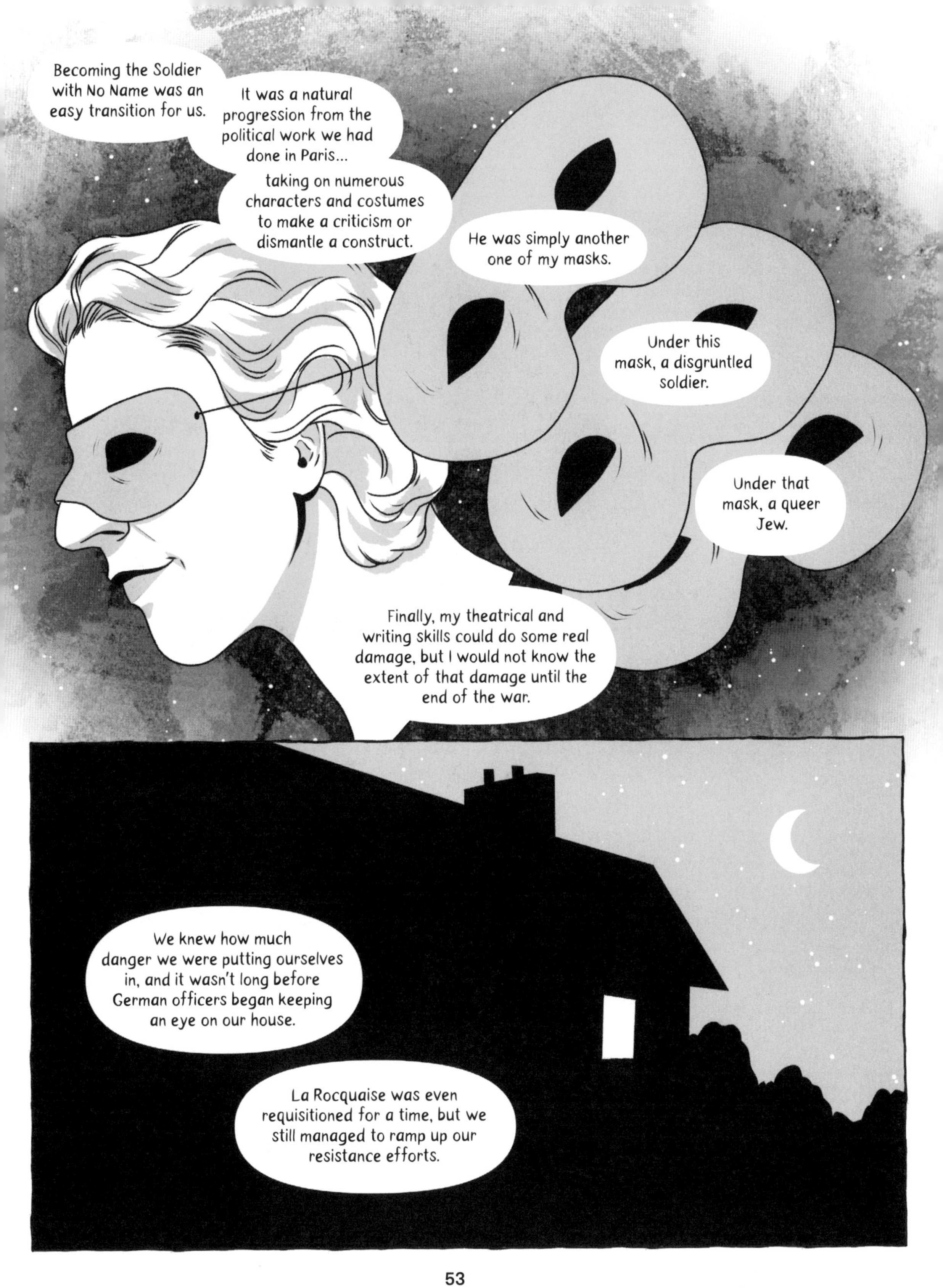

Becoming the Soldier with No Name was an easy transition for us.
It was a natural progression from the political work we had done in Paris...
taking on numerous characters and costumes to make a criticism or dismantle a construct.
He was simply another one of my masks.
Under this mask, a disgruntled soldier.
Under that mask, a queer Jew.
Finally, my theatrical and writing skills could do some real damage, but I would not know the extent of that damage until the end of the war.
We knew how much danger we were putting ourselves in, and it wasn't long before German officers began keeping an eye on our house.
La Rocquaise was even requisitioned for a time, but we still managed to ramp up our resistance efforts.

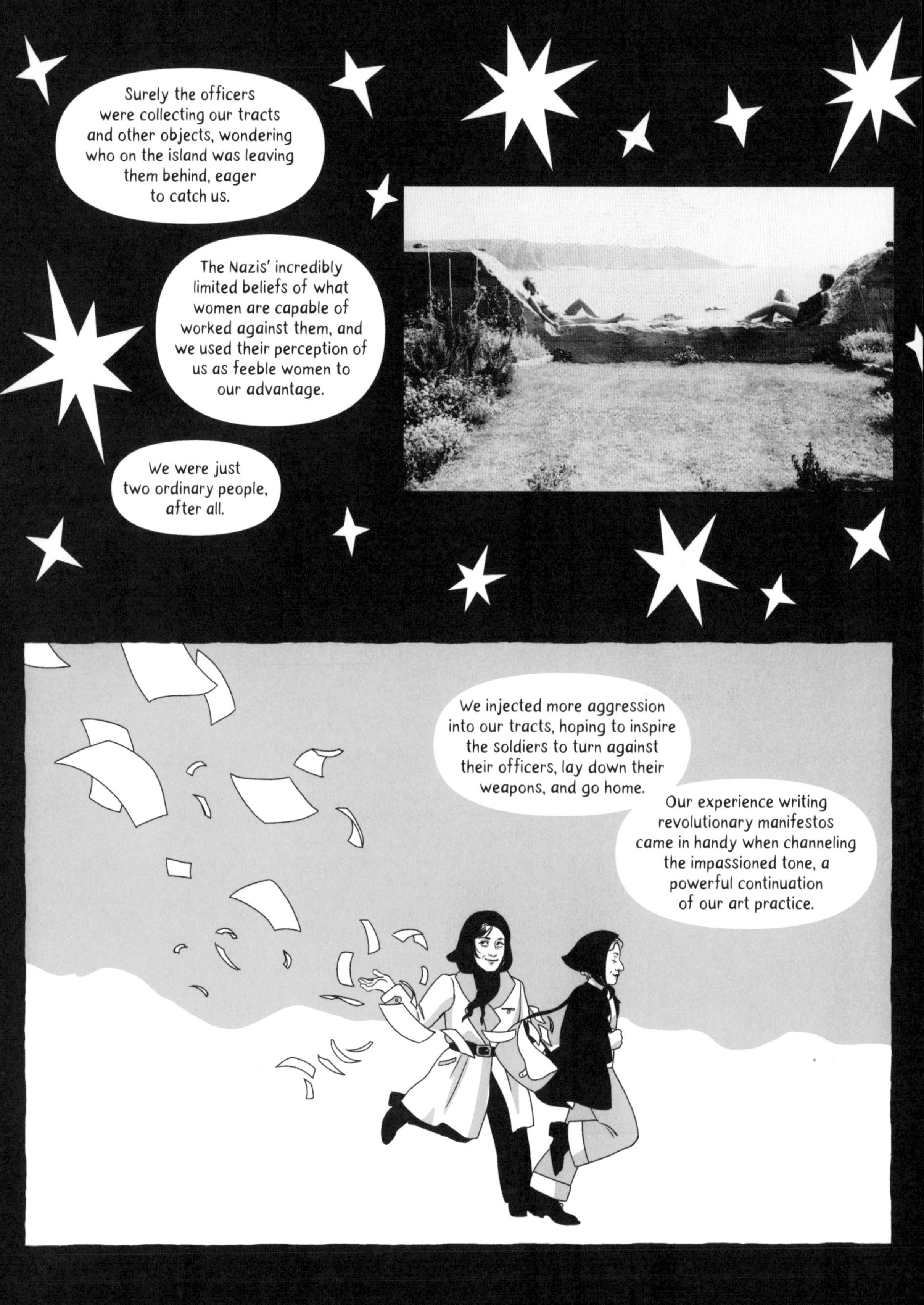
Surely the officers were collecting our tracts and other objects, wondering who on the island was leaving them behind, eager to catch us.
The Nazis' incredibly limited beliefs of what women are capable of worked against them, and we used their perception of us as feeble women to our advantage.
We were just two ordinary people, after all.
We injected more aggression into our tracts, hoping to inspire the soldiers to turn against their officers, lay down their weapons, and go home.
Our experience writing revolutionary manifestos came in handy when channeling the impassioned tone, a powerful continuation of our art practice.

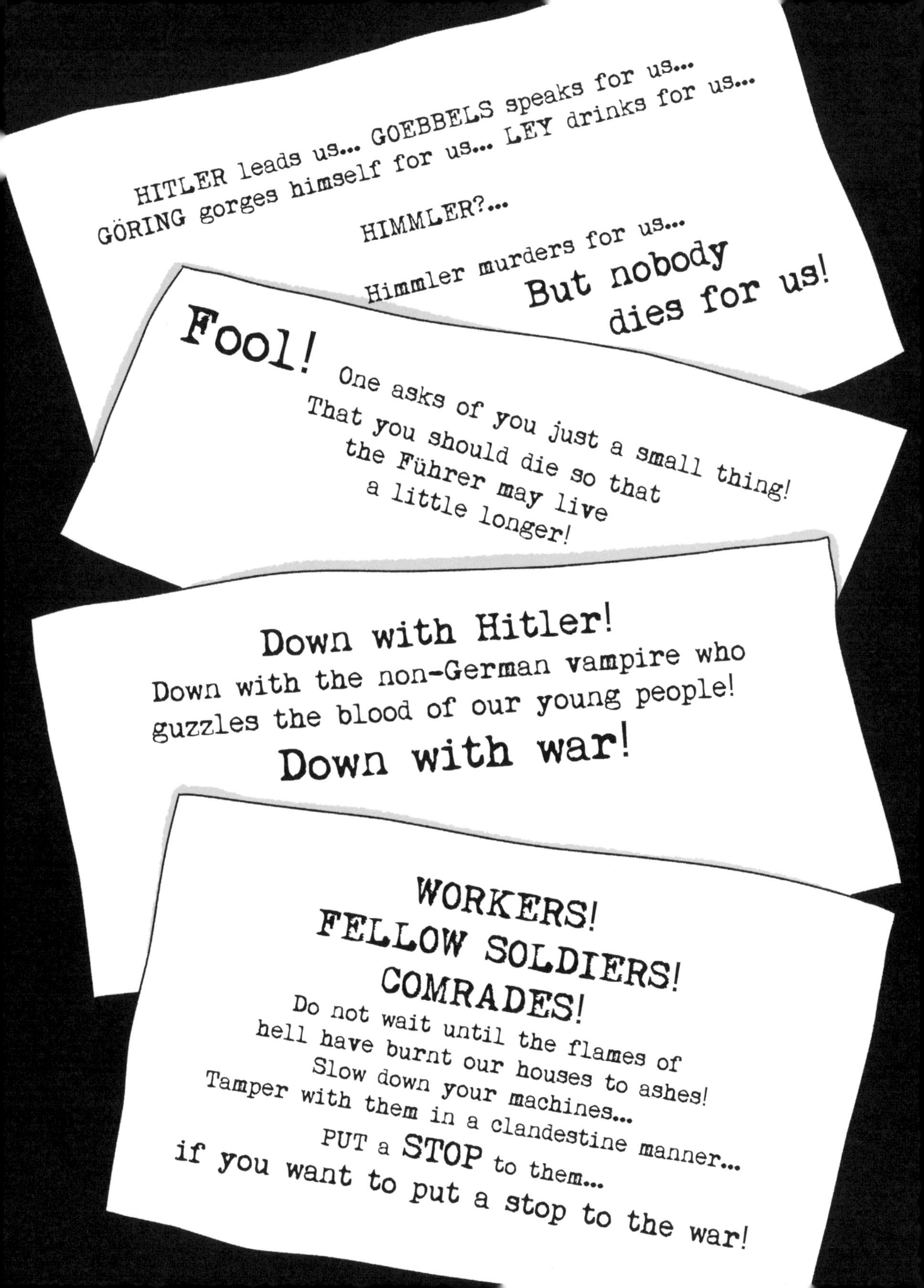
HITLER leads us... GOEBBELS speaks for us...
GÖRING gorges himself for us... LEY drinks for us...
HIMMLER?...
Himmler murders for us...
But nobody dies for us!
Fool! One asks of you just a small thing!
That you should die so that
the Führer may live
a little longer!
Down with Hitler!
Down with the non-German vampire who
guzzles the blood of our young people!
Down with war!
WORKERS!
FELLOW SOLDIERS!
COMRADES!
Do not wait until the flames of
hell have burnt our houses to ashes!
Slow down your machines...
Tamper with them in a clandestine manner...
PUT a STOP to them...
if you want to put a stop to the war!

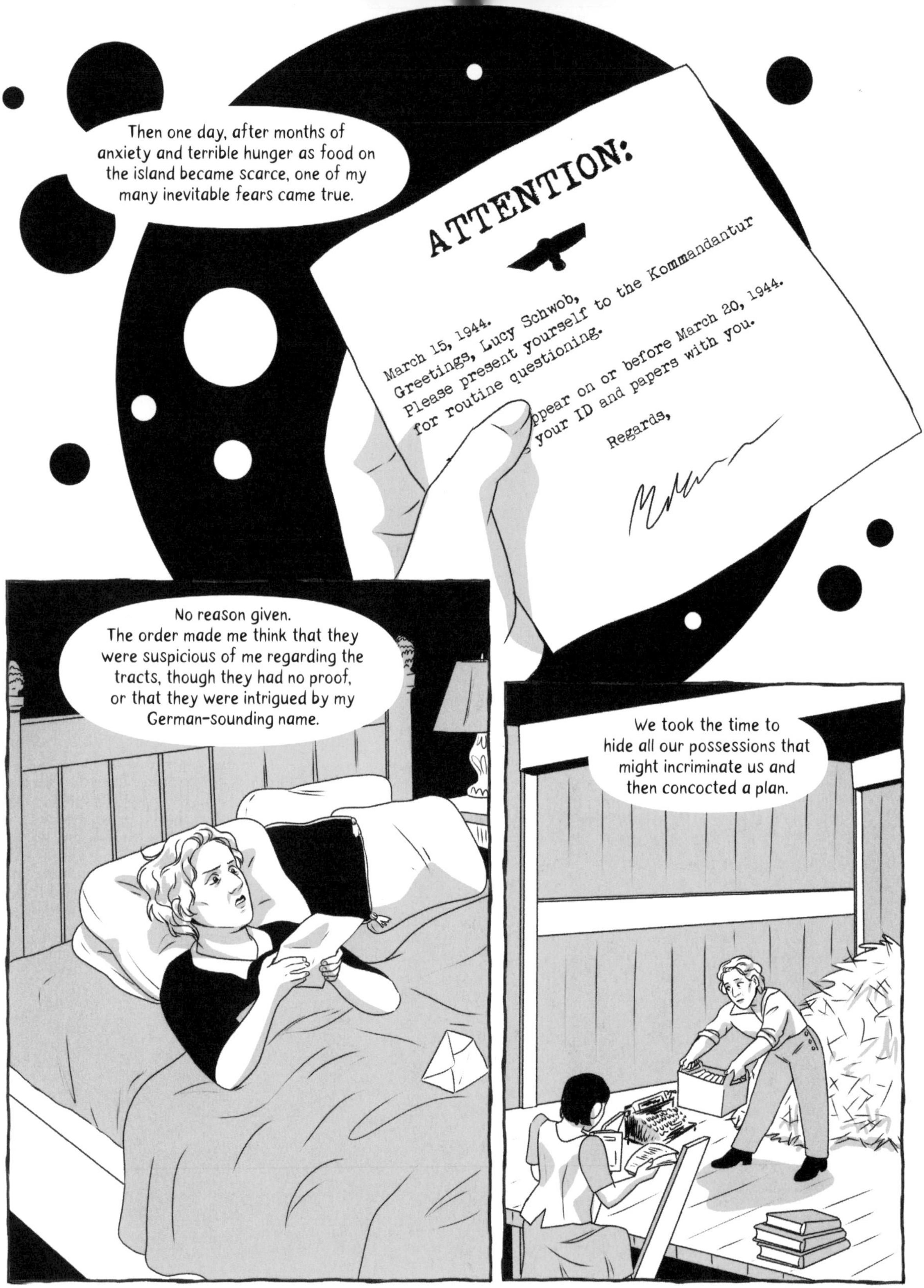
Then one day, after months of anxiety and terrible hunger as food on the island became scarce, one of my many inevitable fears came true.
ATTENTION:
March 15, 1944.
Greetings, Lucy Schwob,
Please present yourself to the Kommandantur for routine questioning.
ppear on or before March 20, 1944.
your ID and papers with you.
Regards,
No reason given.
The order made me think that they were suspicious of me regarding the tracts, though they had no proof, or that they were intrigued by my German-sounding name.
We took the time to hide all our possessions that might incriminate us and then concocted a plan.

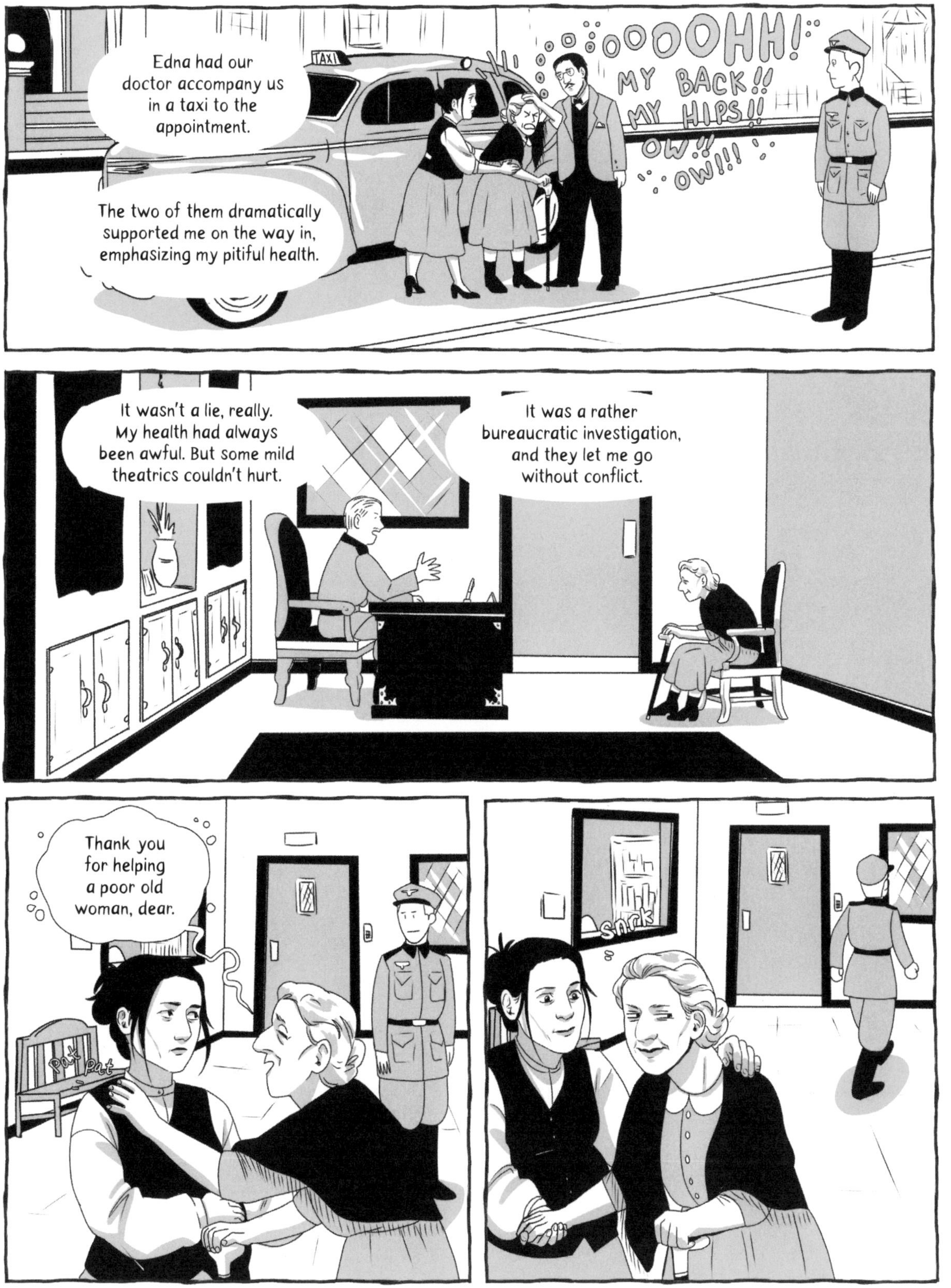
Edna had our doctor accompany us in a taxi to the appointment.
TAXI
OOOOHH!
MY BACK!!
MY HIPS!!
OW!!
OW!!!
The two of them dramatically supported me on the way in, emphasizing my pitiful health.
It wasn't a lie, really. My health had always been awful. But some mild theatrics couldn't hurt.
It was a rather bureaucratic investigation, and they let me go without conflict.
Thank you for helping a poor old woman, dear.
pat pat

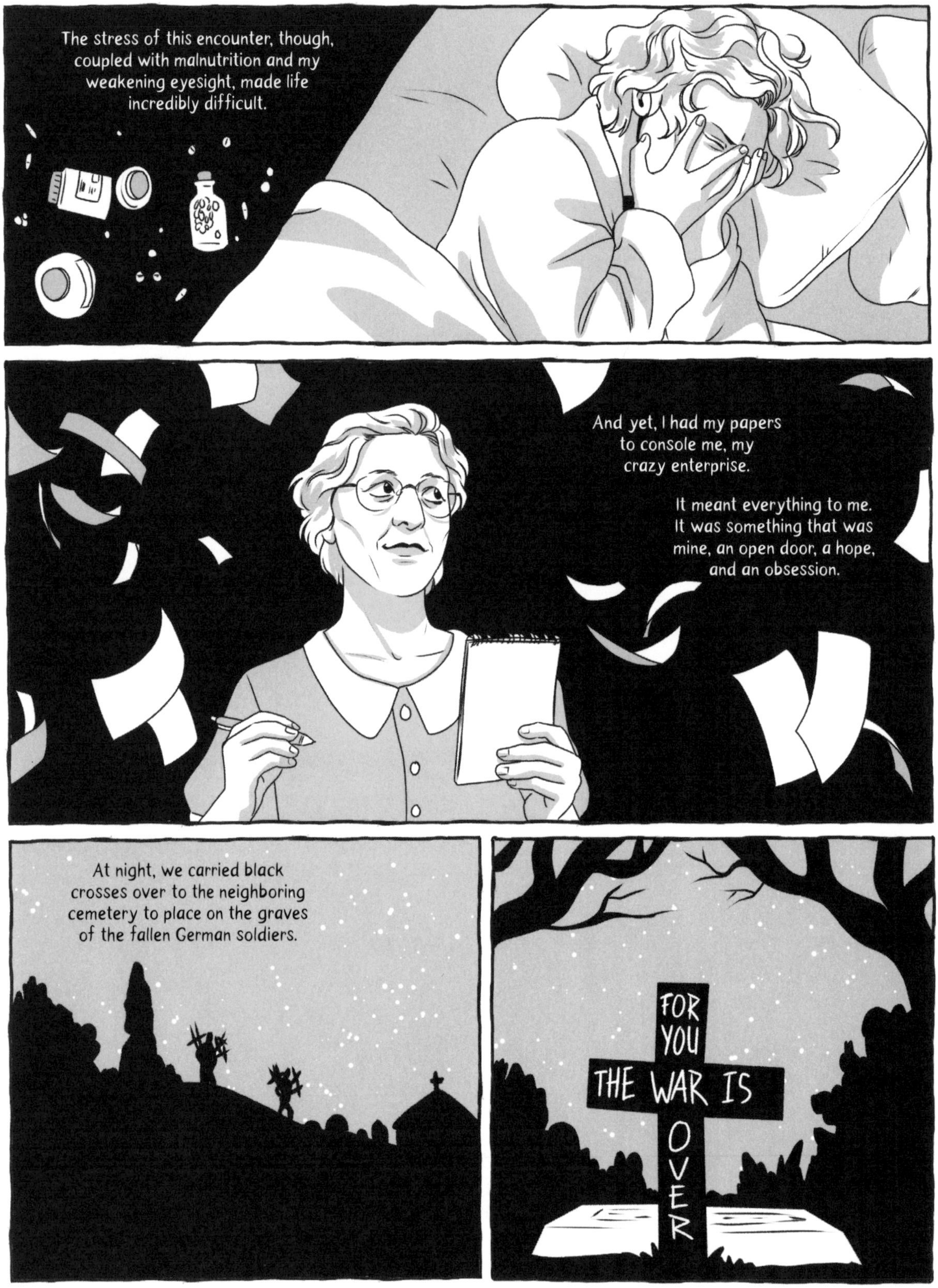
The stress of this encounter, though, coupled with malnutrition and my weakening eyesight, made life incredibly difficult.
And yet, I had my papers to console me, my crazy enterprise.
It meant everything to me. It was something that was mine, an open door, a hope, and an obsession.
At night, we carried black crosses over to the neighboring cemetery to place on the graves of the fallen German soldiers.
FOR YOU THE WAR IS OVER

Then the day came when our luck ran out.

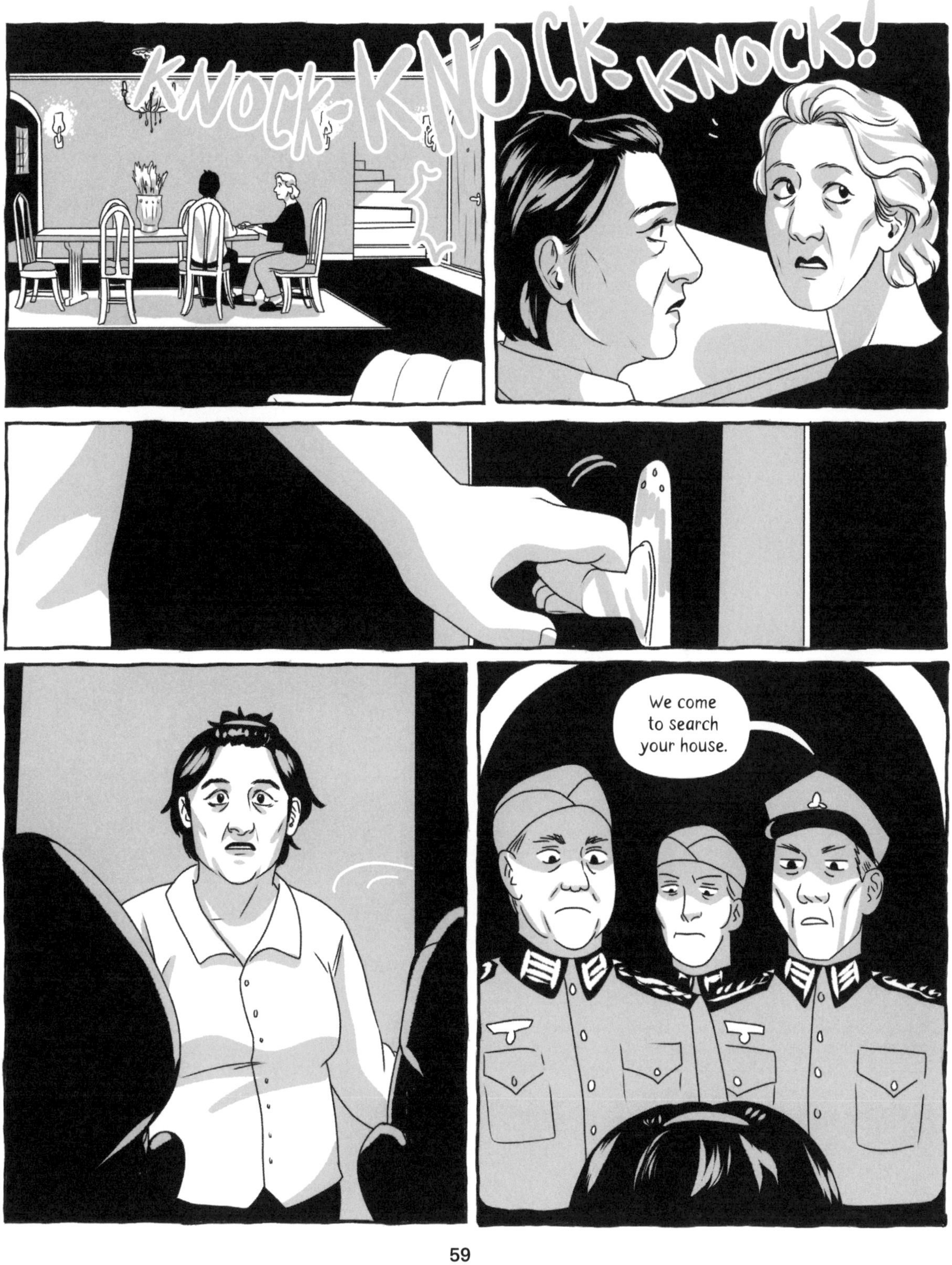
KNOCK-KNOCK-KNOCK!
We come to search your house.

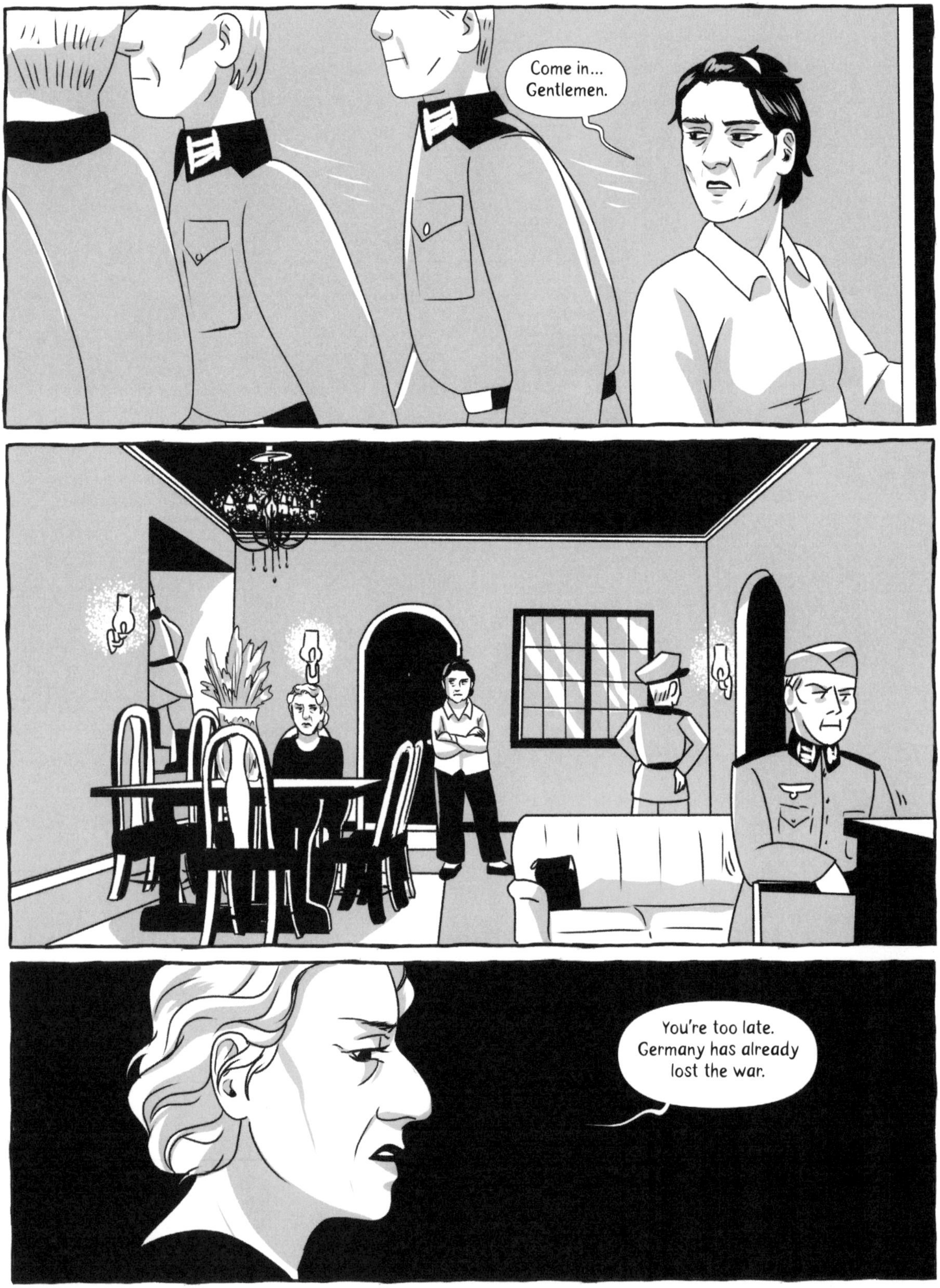
Come in... Gentlemen.
You're too late. Germany has already lost the war.

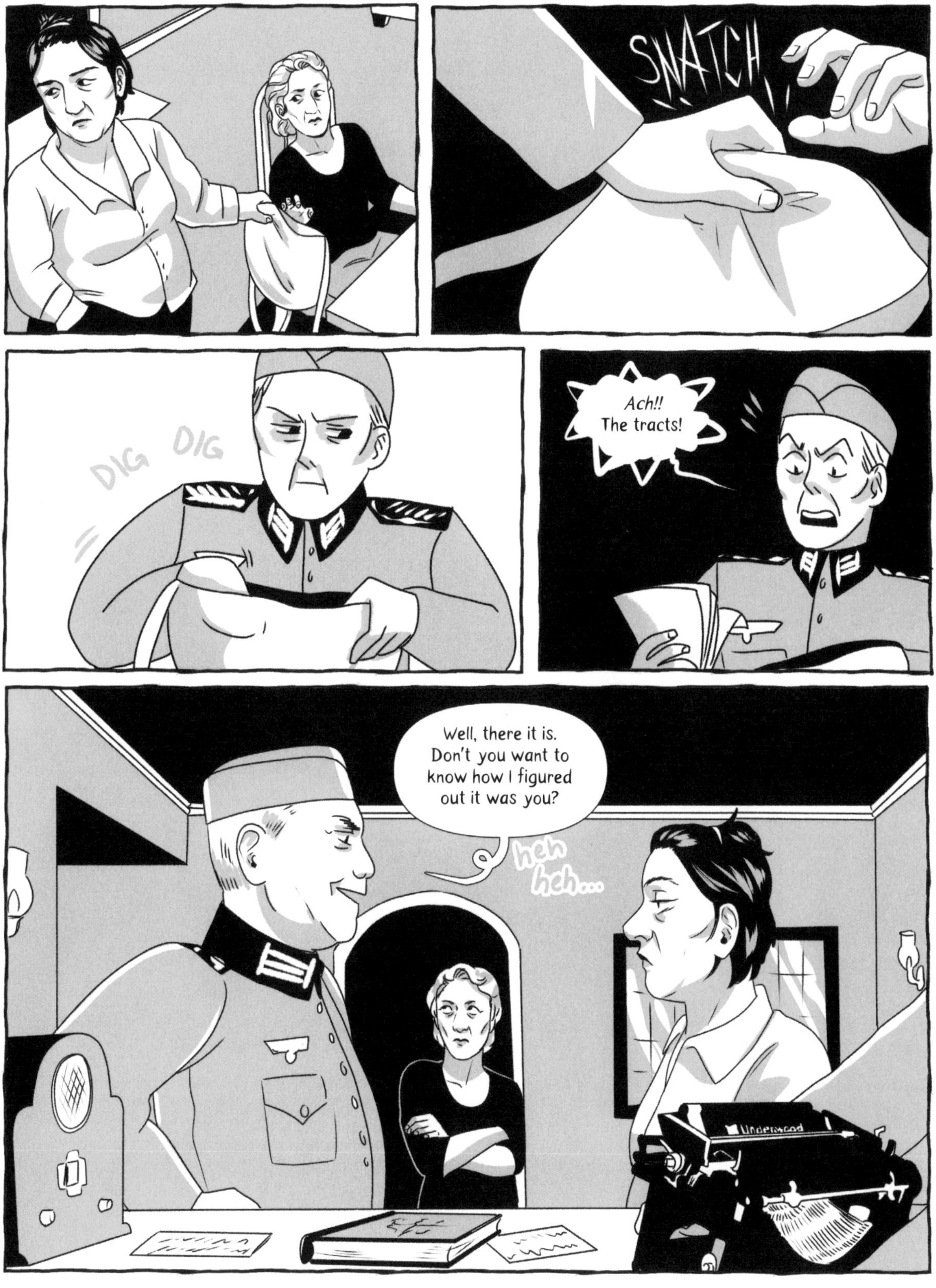
SNATCH
DIG DIG
Ach!! The tracts!
Well, there it is. Don't you want to know how I figured out it was you?
heh heh...
Underwood

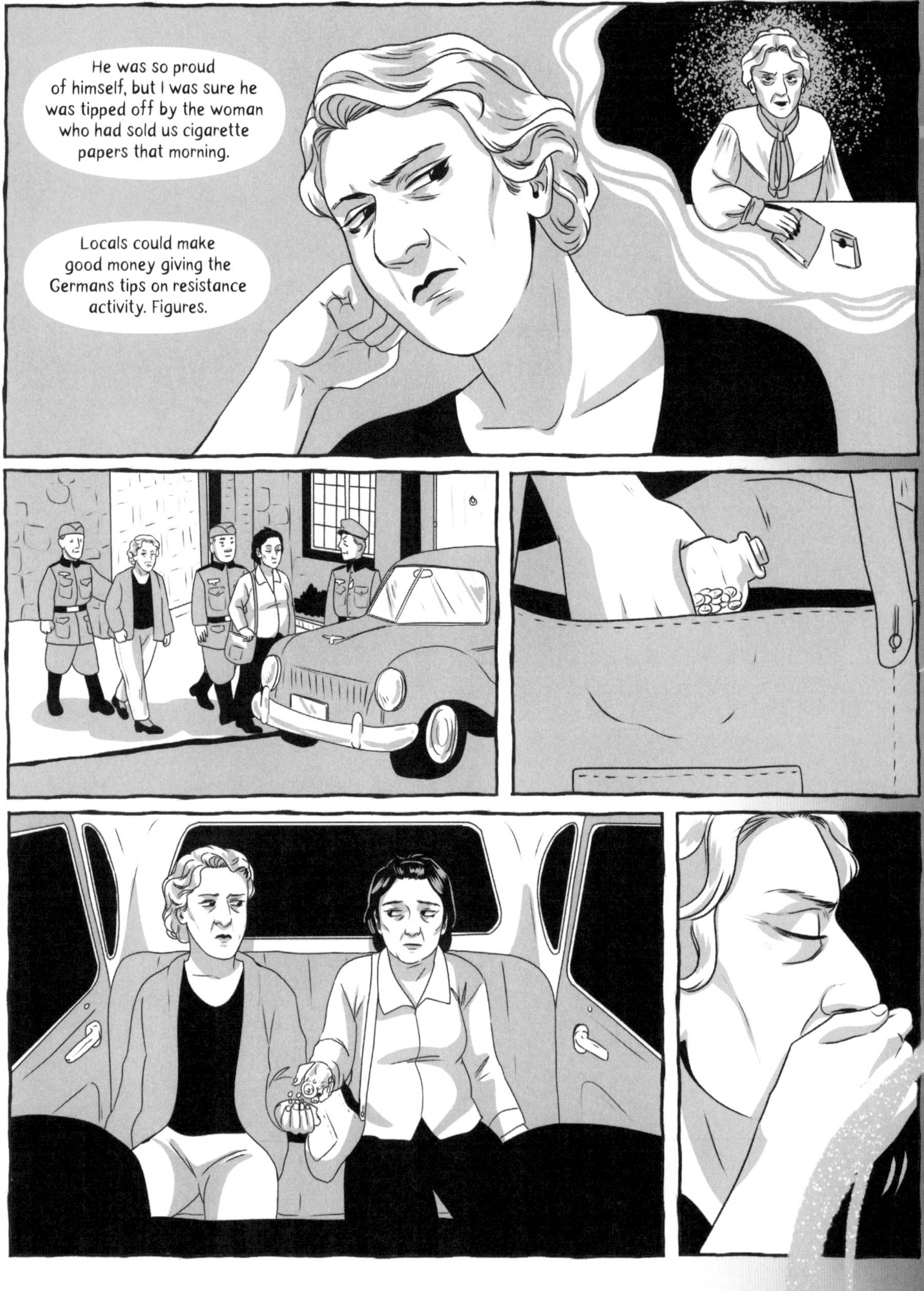
He was so proud of himself, but I was sure he was tipped off by the woman who had sold us cigarette papers that morning.
Locals could make good money giving the Germans tips on resistance activity. Figures.

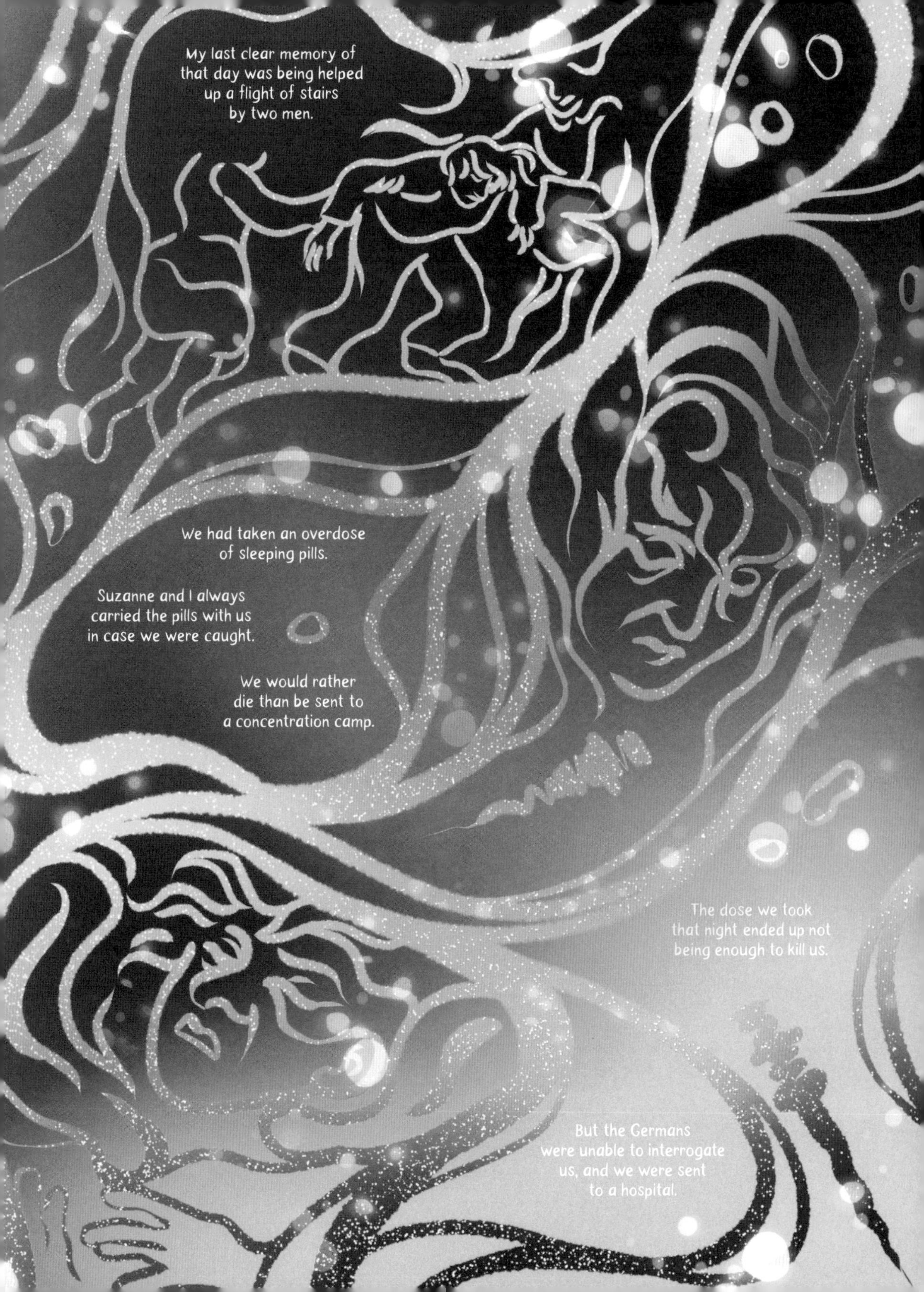
My last clear memory of that day was being helped up a flight of stairs by two men.
We had taken an overdose of sleeping pills.
Suzanne and I always carried the pills with us in case we were caught.
We would rather die than be sent to a concentration camp.
The dose we took that night ended up not being enough to kill us.
But the Germans were unable to interrogate us, and we were sent to a hospital.

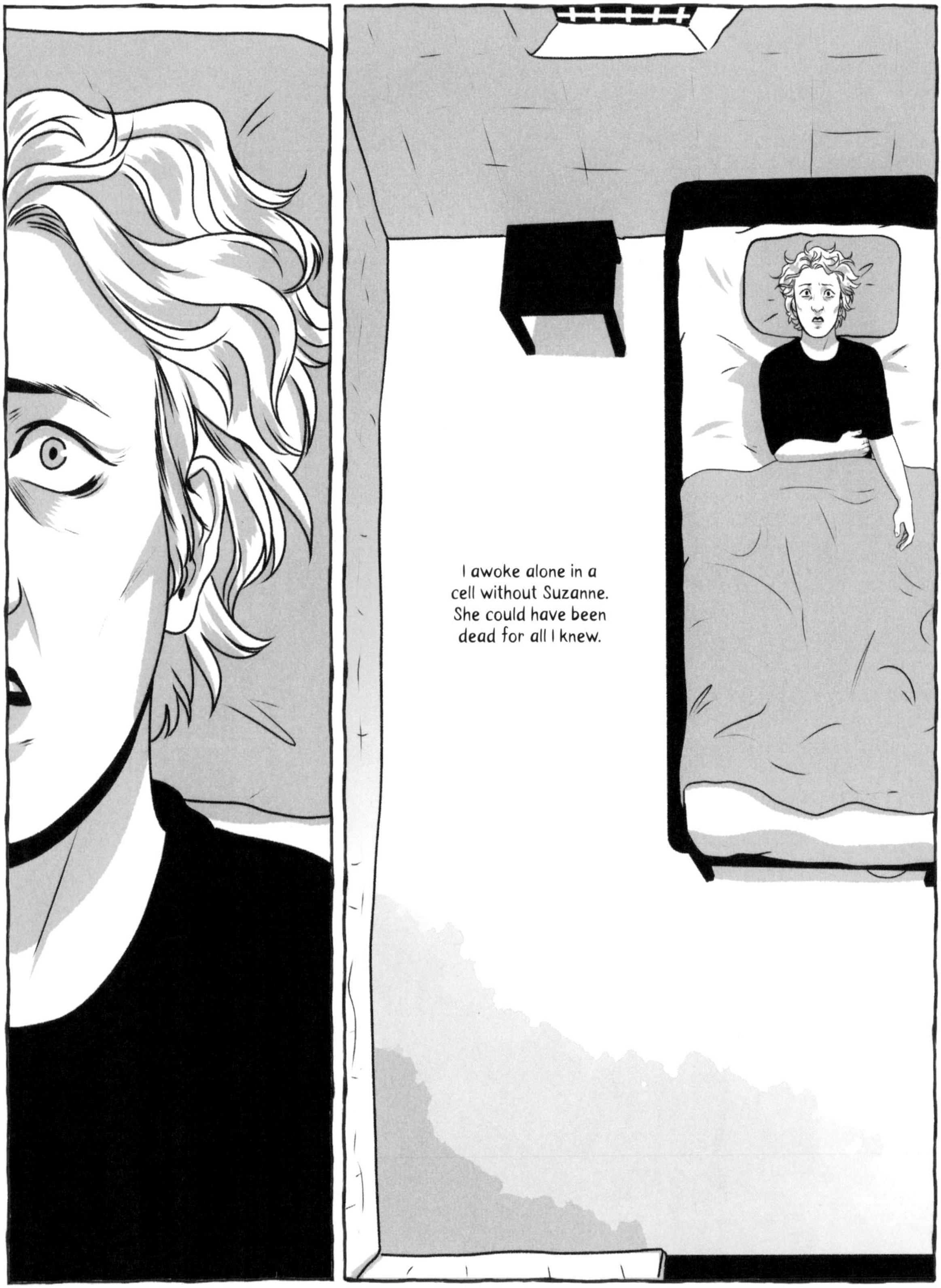
I awoke alone in a cell without Suzanne. She could have been dead for all I knew.

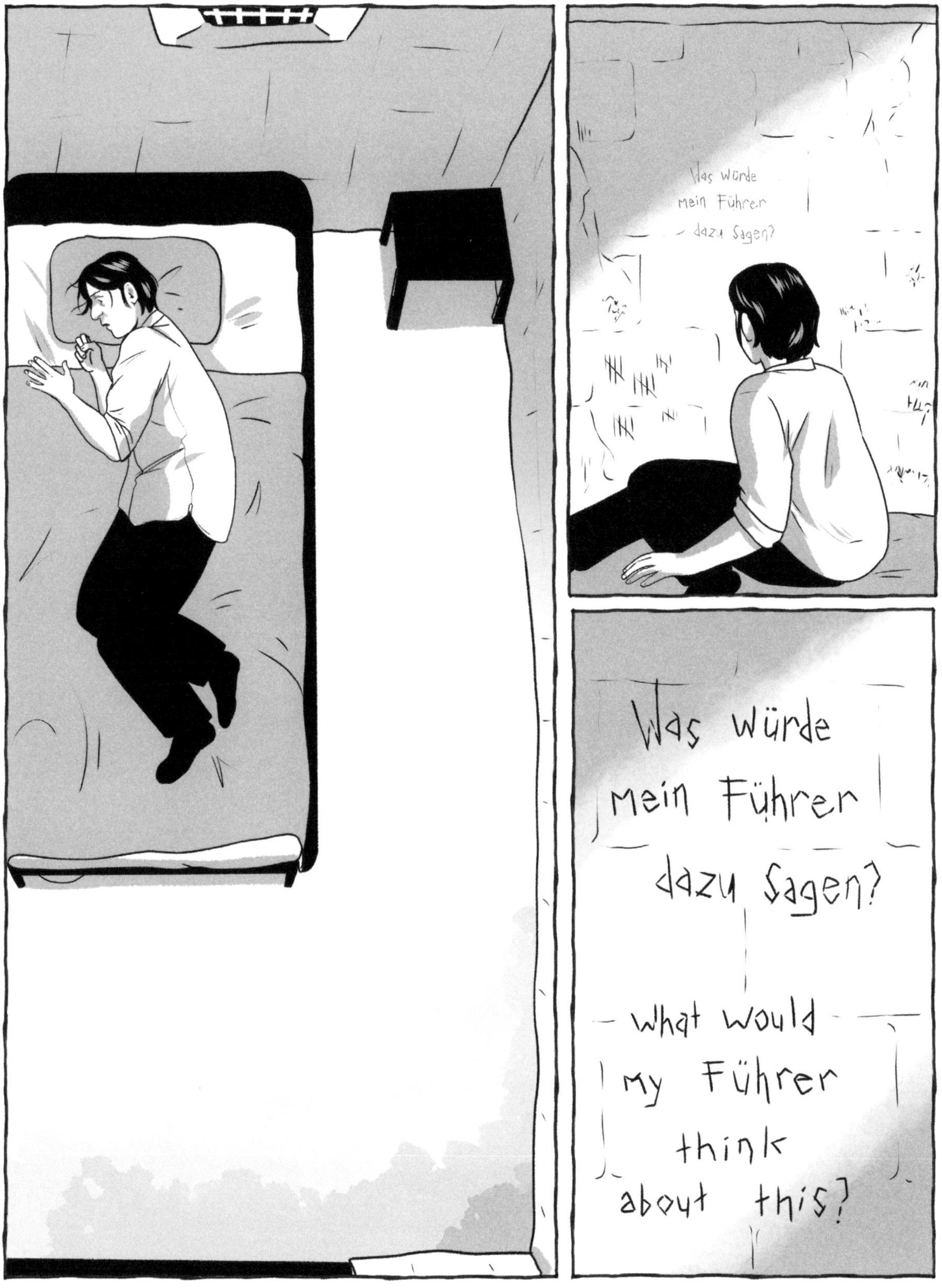
Was würde mein Führer dazu Sagen?
Was würde mein Führer dazu Sagen?
what would my Führer think about this?

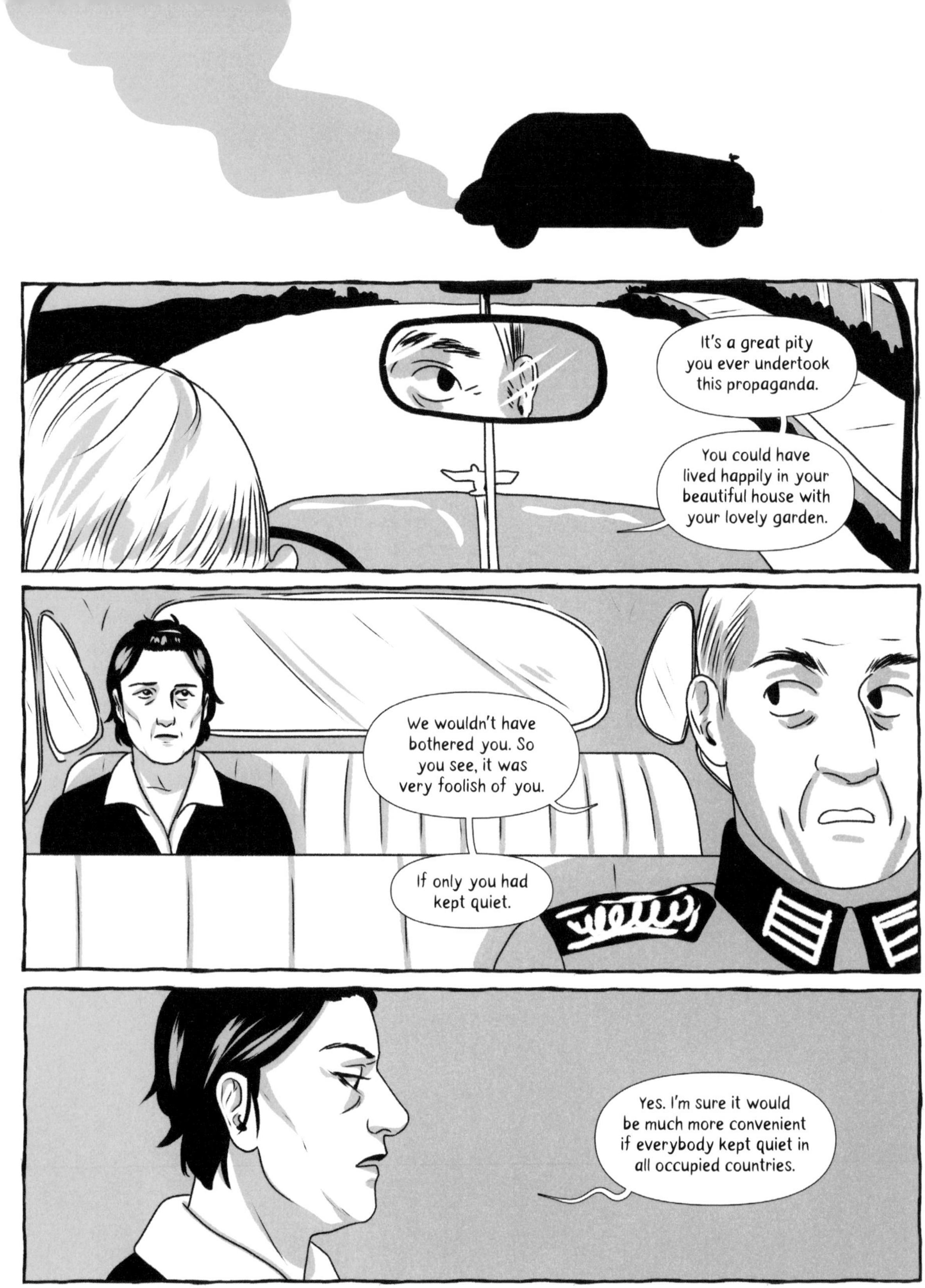
It's a great pity you ever undertook this propaganda.
You could have lived happily in your beautiful house with your lovely garden.
We wouldn't have bothered you. So you see, it was very foolish of you.
If only you had kept quiet.
Yes. I'm sure it would be much more convenient if everybody kept quiet in all occupied countries.

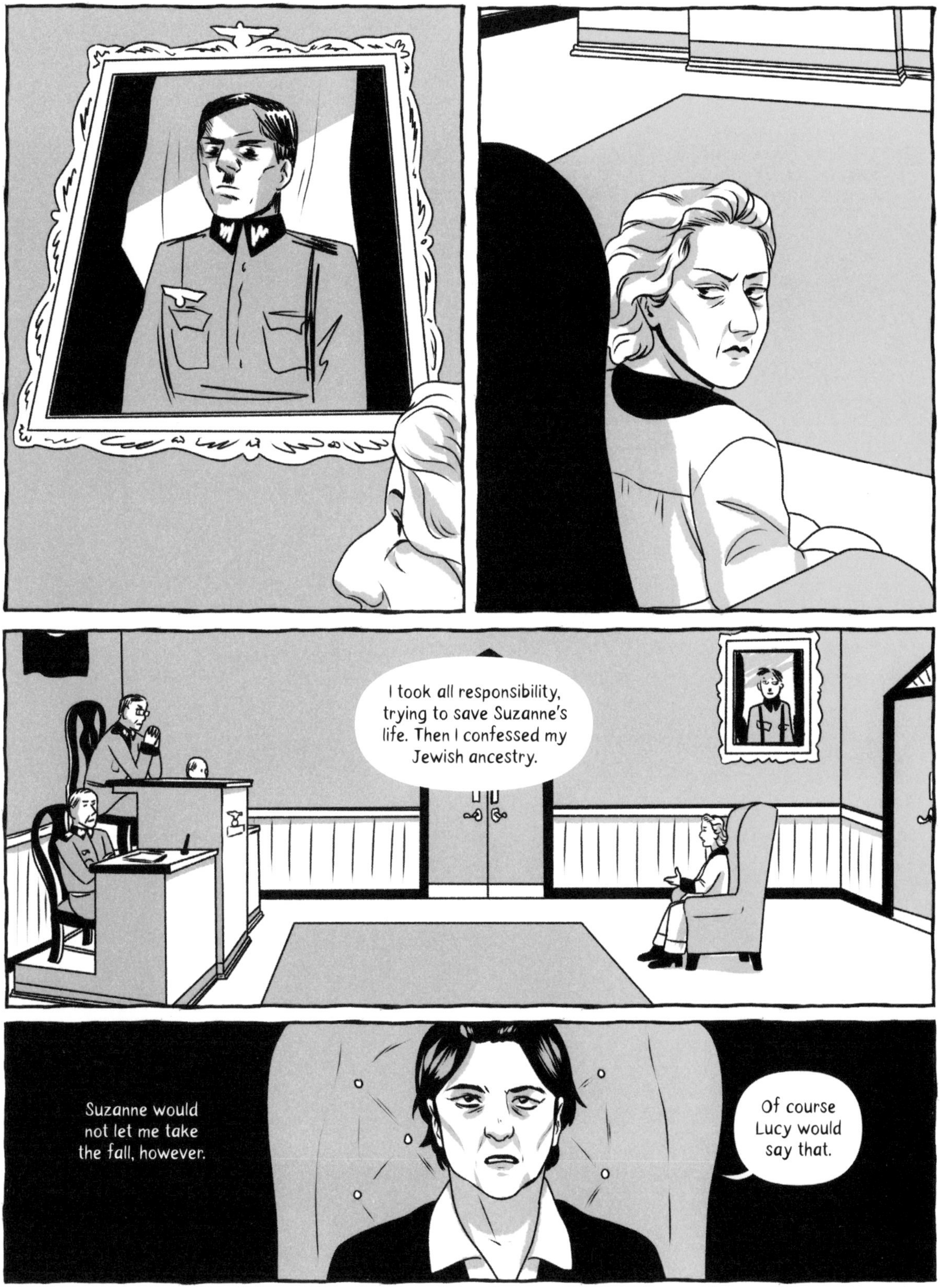
I took all responsibility, trying to save Suzanne's life. Then I confessed my Jewish ancestry.
Suzanne would not let me take the fall, however.
Of course Lucy would say that.

But when it comes to two people who have worked together since adolescence, discussing everything,

it's impossible to trace the source of an idea to only one or the other.

Isolation from each other was torture.

I loved Suzanne's laugh; for me, it was one of a kind. I thought of her every day until our trial.

But we managed to smuggle notes to each other through the secret postal system the other inmates had set up.

Her notes kept my soul alive.

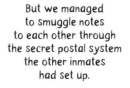

Amour,
Stay Strong ♡
Amour,
♡ All my love
Amour,
Goodnight.
Courage. Love. ♡

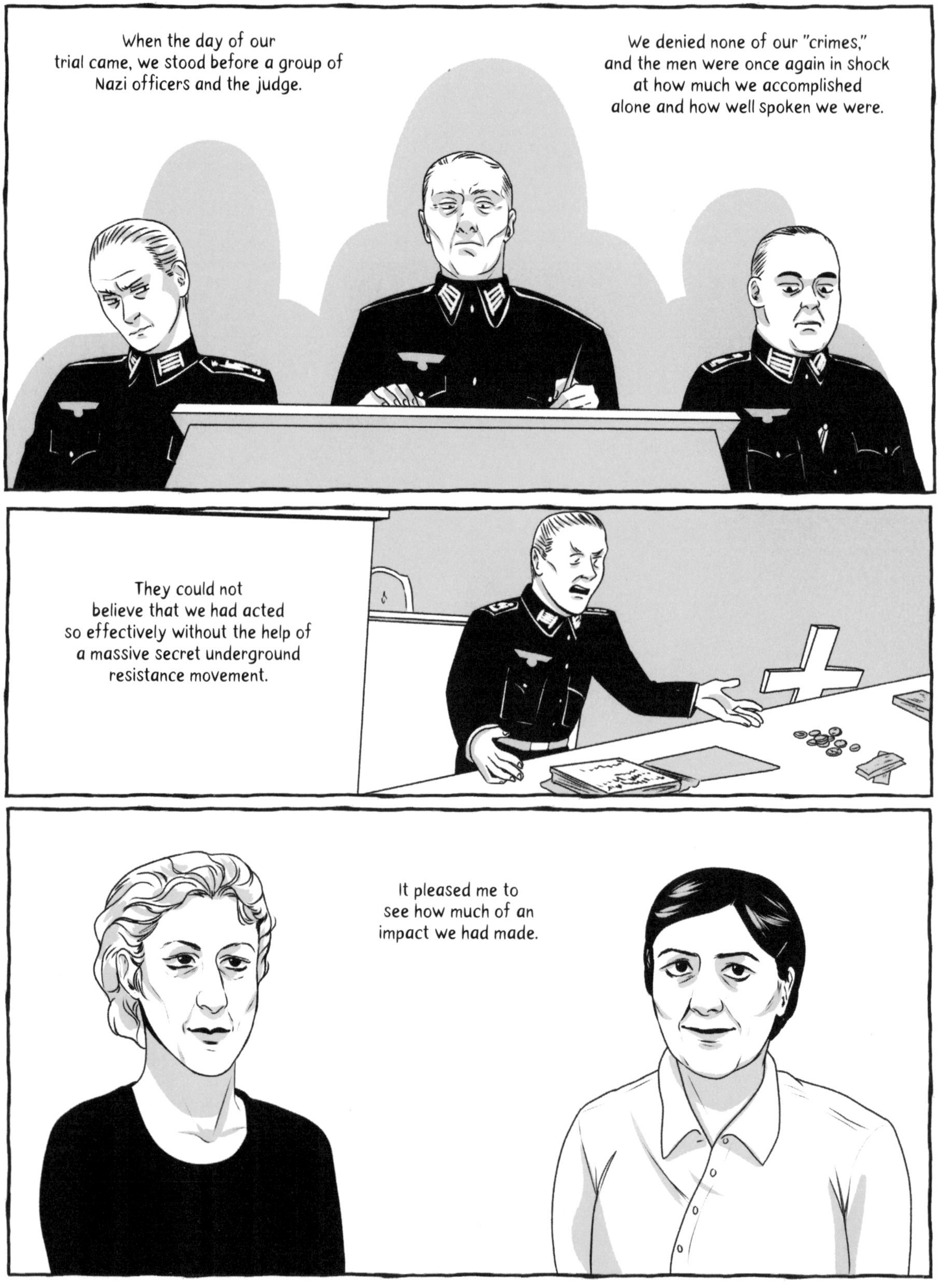
When the day of our trial came, we stood before a group of Nazi officers and the judge.
We denied none of our "crimes," and the men were once again in shock at how much we accomplished alone and how well spoken we were.
They could not believe that we had acted so effectively without the help of a massive secret underground resistance movement.
It pleased me to see how much of an impact we had made.

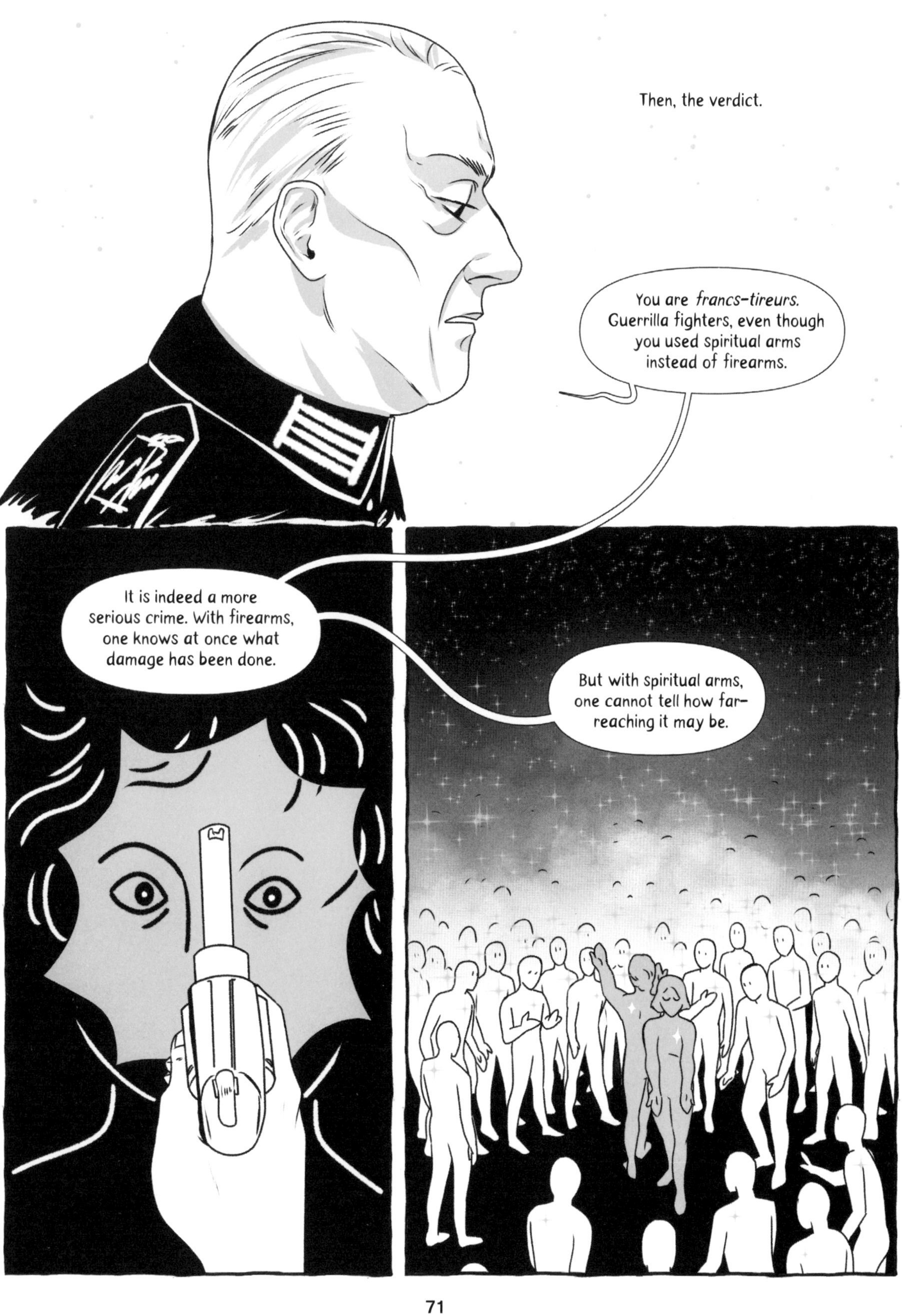
Then, the verdict.
You are *francs-tireurs.* Guerrilla fighters, even though you used spiritual arms instead of firearms.
It is indeed a more serious crime. With firearms, one knows at once what damage has been done.
But with spiritual arms, one cannot tell how far-reaching it may be.

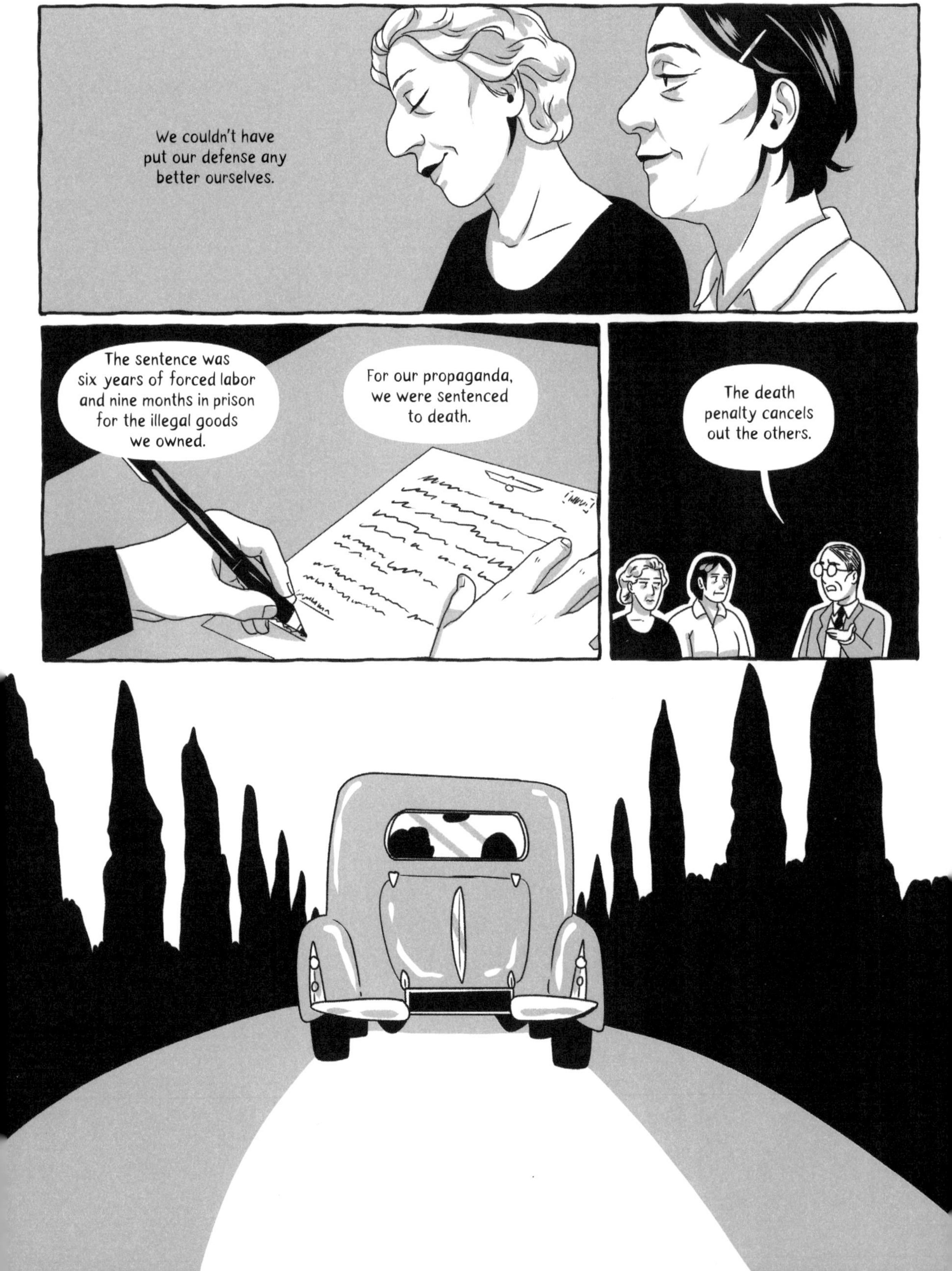
We couldn't have put our defense any better ourselves.
The sentence was six years of forced labor and nine months in prison for the illegal goods we owned.
For our propaganda, we were sentenced to death.
The death penalty cancels out the others.

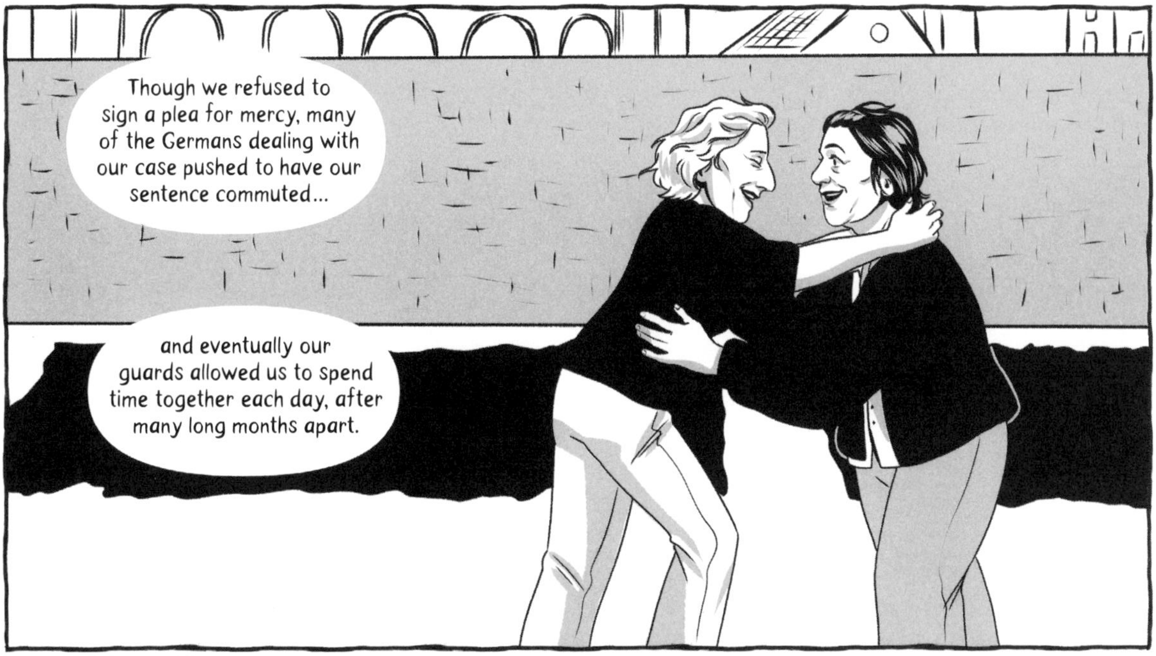
Though we refused to sign a plea for mercy, many of the Germans dealing with our case pushed to have our sentence commuted...
and eventually our guards allowed us to spend time together each day, after many long months apart.

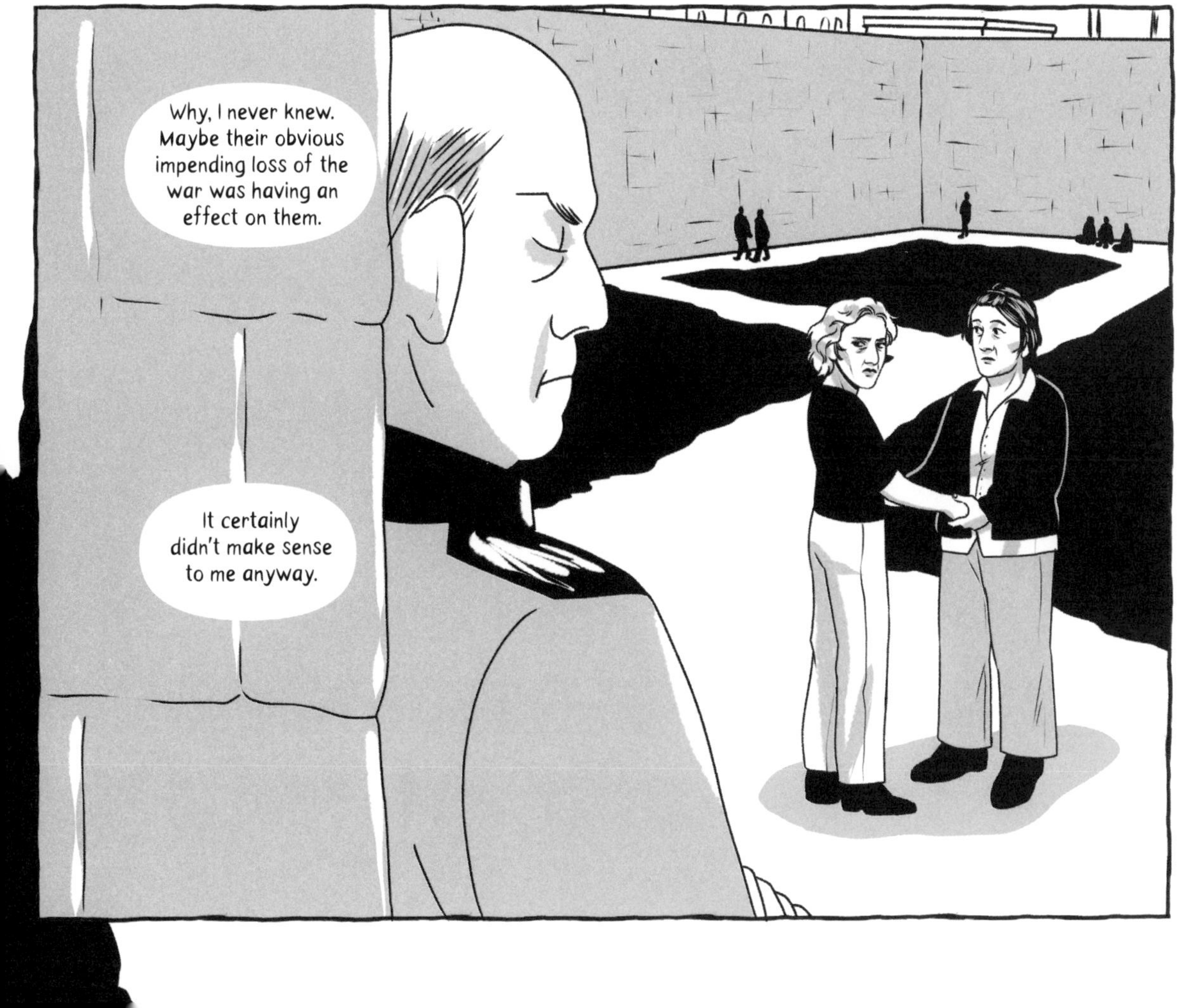
Why, I never knew. Maybe their obvious impending loss of the war was having an effect on them.
It certainly didn't make sense to me anyway.

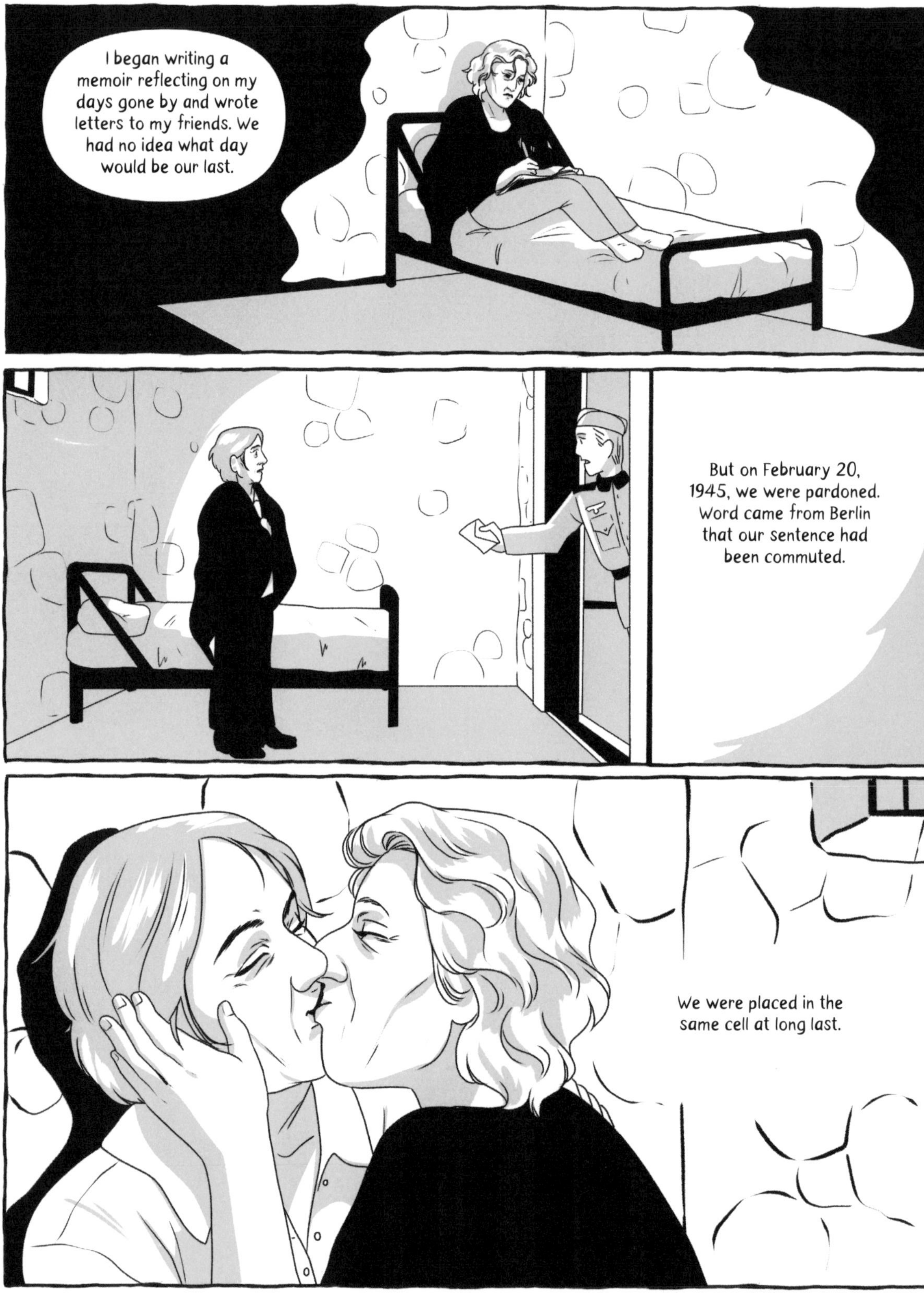
I began writing a memoir reflecting on my days gone by and wrote letters to my friends. We had no idea what day would be our last.
But on February 20, 1945, we were pardoned. Word came from Berlin that our sentence had been commuted.
We were placed in the same cell at long last.

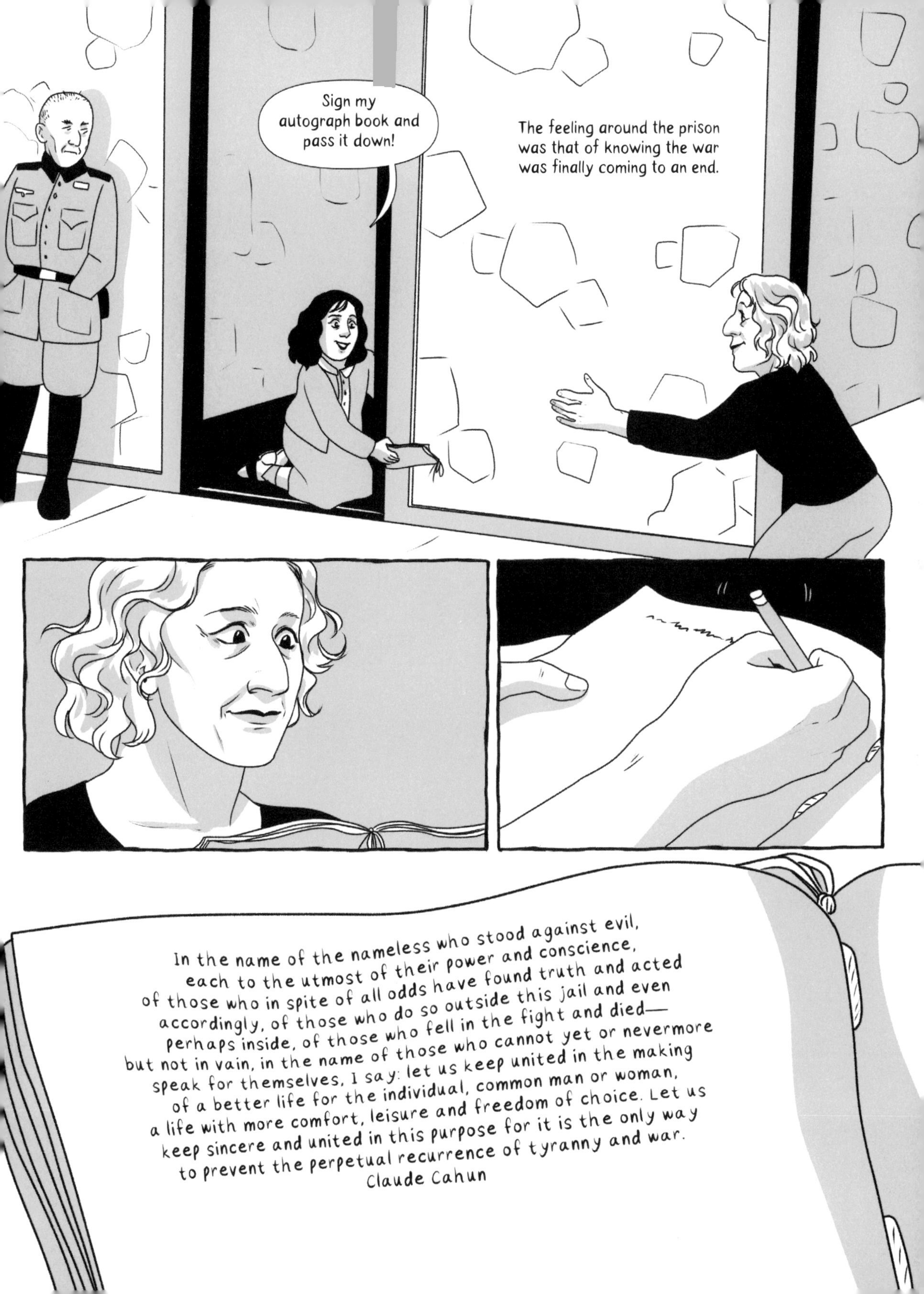
Sign my autograph book and pass it down!
The feeling around the prison was that of knowing the war was finally coming to an end.
In the name of the nameless who stood against evil,
each to the utmost of their power and conscience,
of those who in spite of all odds have found truth and acted
accordingly, of those who do so outside this jail and even
perhaps inside, of those who fell in the fight and died—
but not in vain, in the name of those who cannot yet or nevermore
speak for themselves, I say: let us keep united in the making
of a better life for the individual, common man or woman,
a life with more comfort, leisure and freedom of choice. Let us
keep sincere and united in this purpose for it is the only way
to prevent the perpetual recurrence of tyranny and war.
Claude Cahun

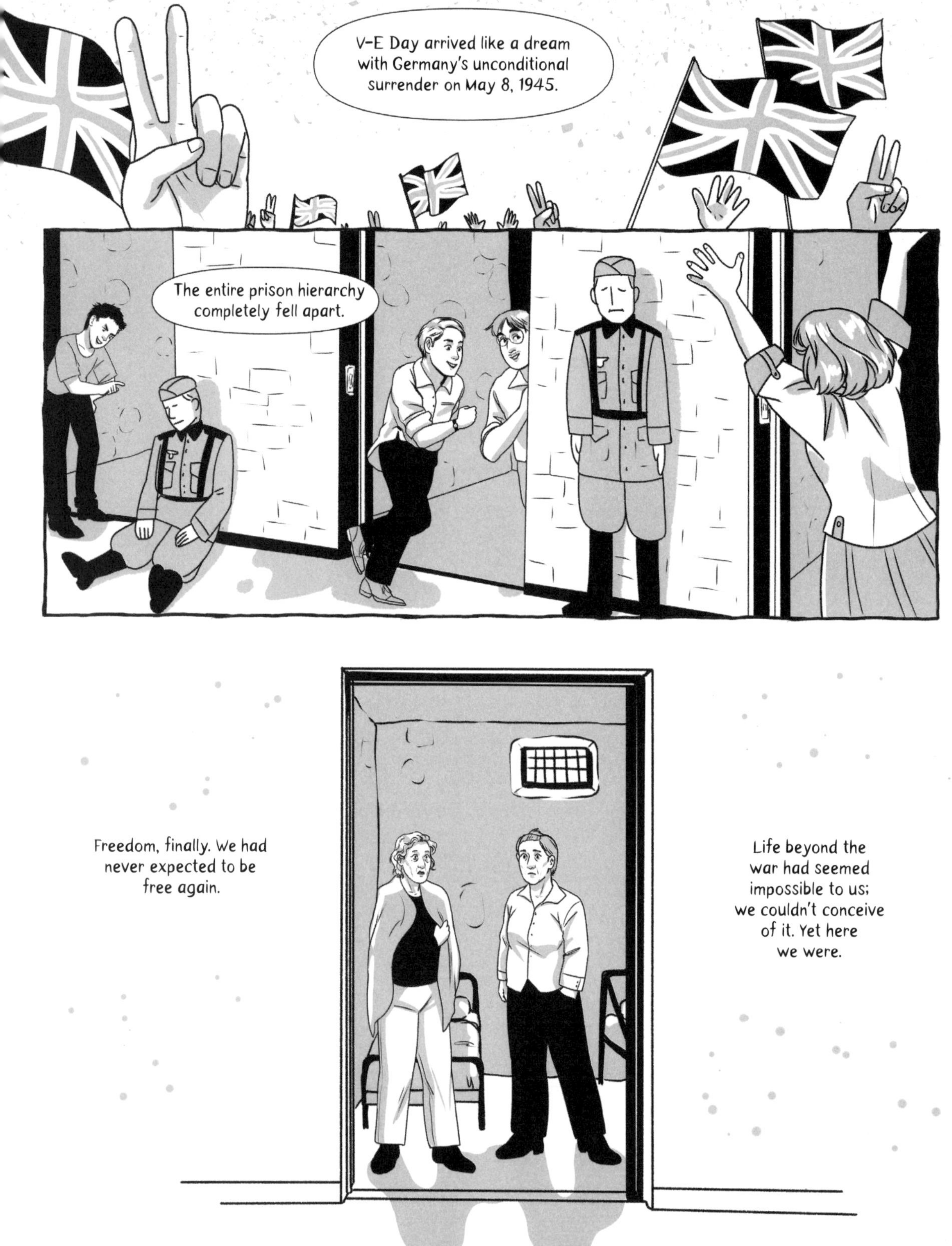
V-E Day arrived like a dream with Germany's unconditional surrender on May 8, 1945.
The entire prison hierarchy completely fell apart.
Freedom, finally. We had never expected to be free again.
Life beyond the war had seemed impossible to us; we couldn't conceive of it. Yet here we were.

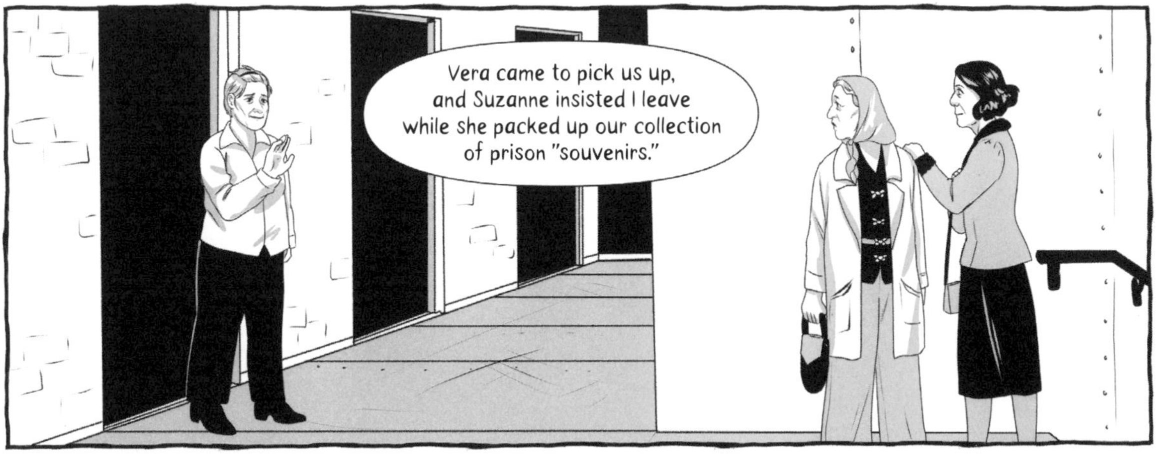
Vera came to pick us up, and Suzanne insisted I leave while she packed up our collection of prison "souvenirs."

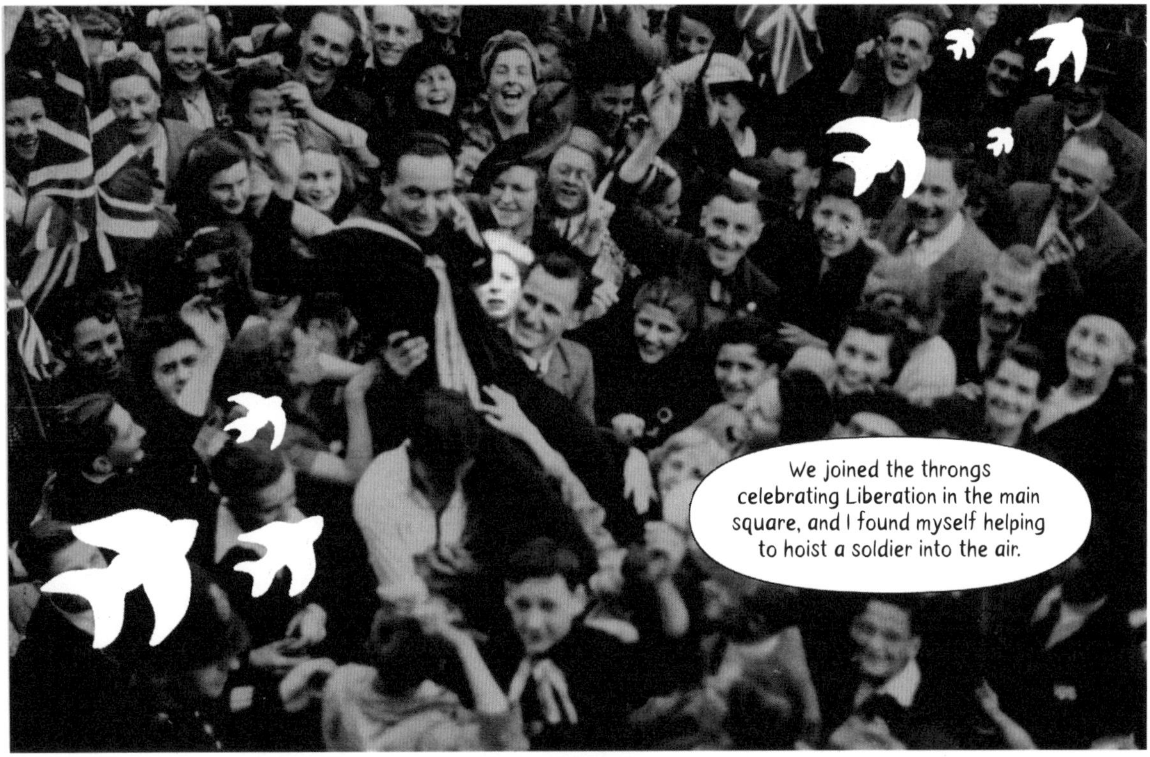
We joined the throngs celebrating Liberation in the main square, and I found myself helping to hoist a soldier into the air.

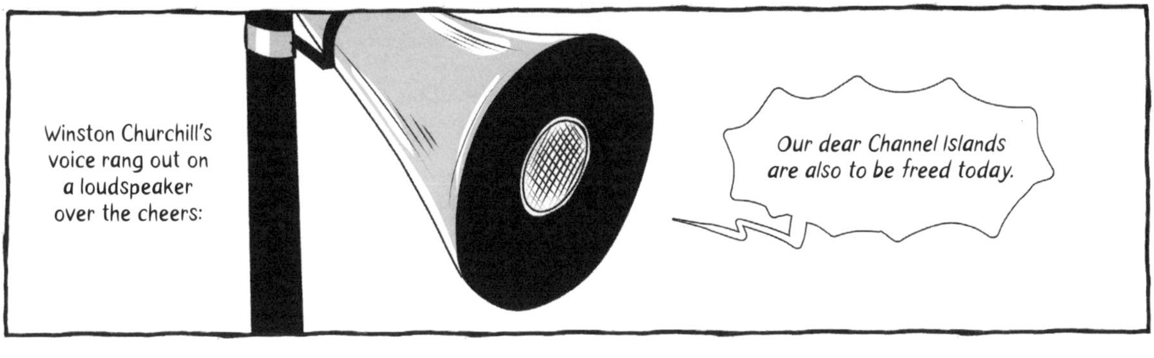
Winston Churchill's voice rang out on a loudspeaker over the cheers:
Our dear Channel Islands are also to be freed today.

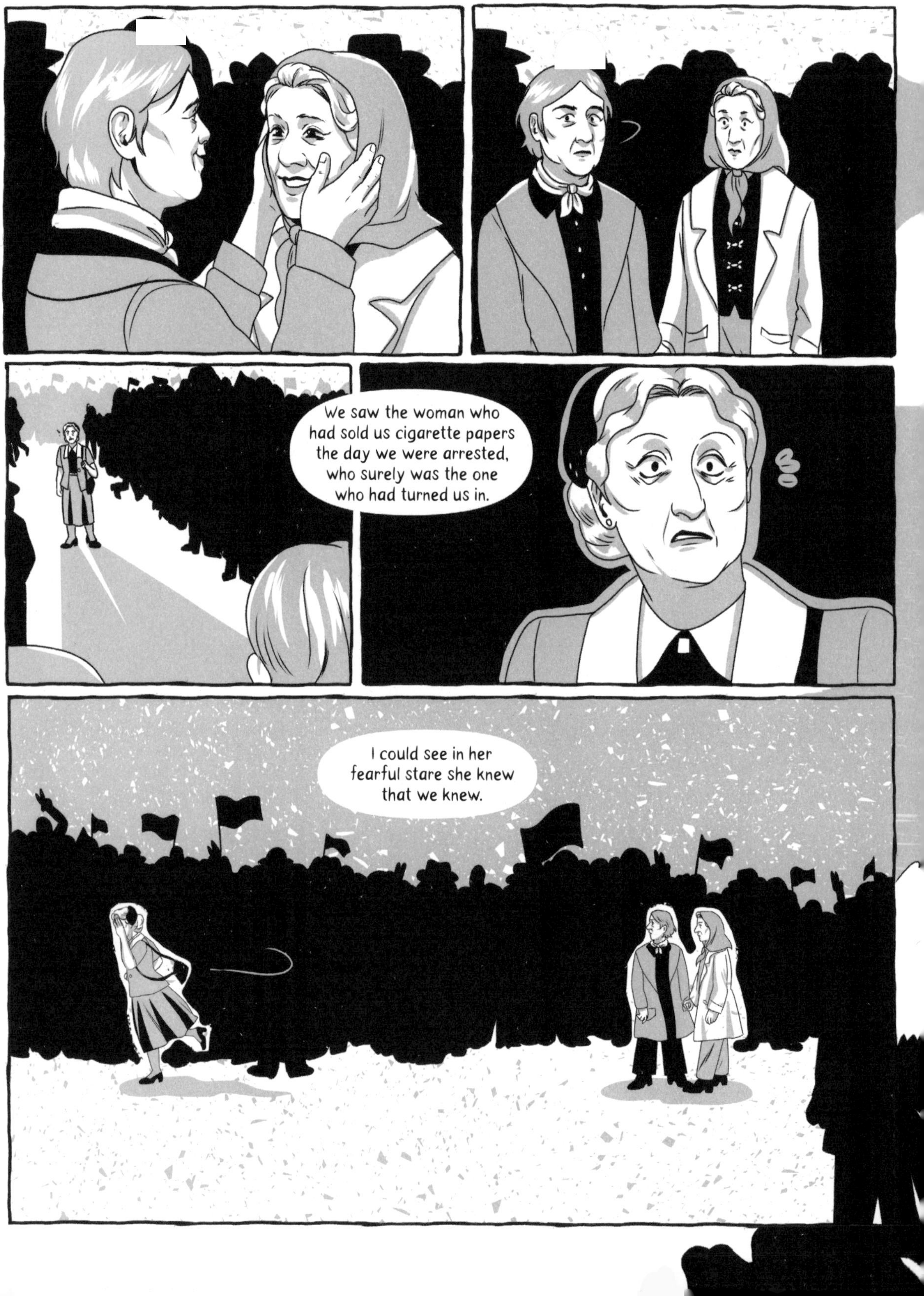
We saw the woman who had sold us cigarette papers the day we were arrested, who surely was the one who had turned us in.
I could see in her fearful stare she knew that we knew.

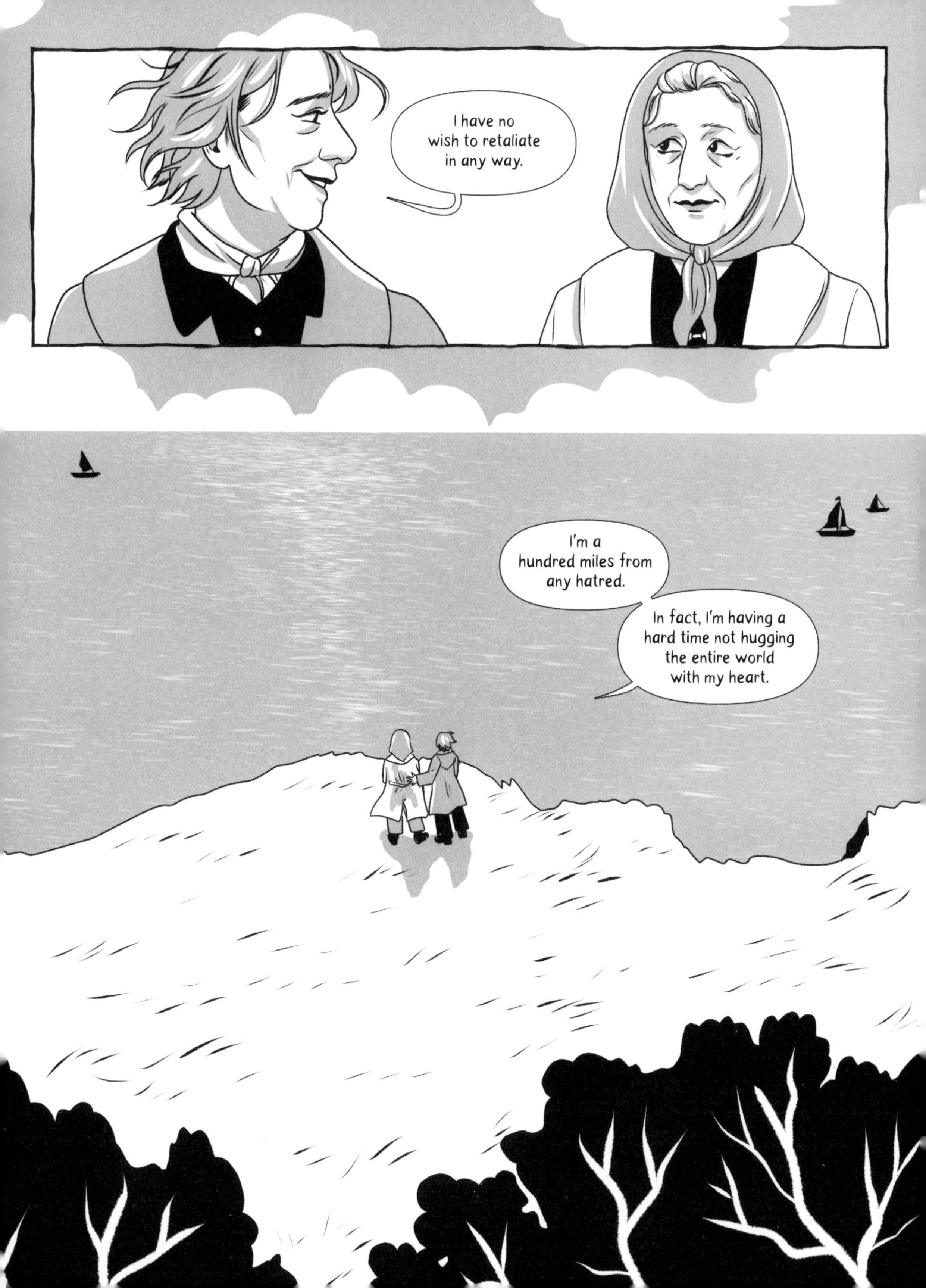
I have no wish to retaliate in any way.
I'm a hundred miles from any hatred.
In fact, I'm having a hard time not hugging the entire world with my heart.

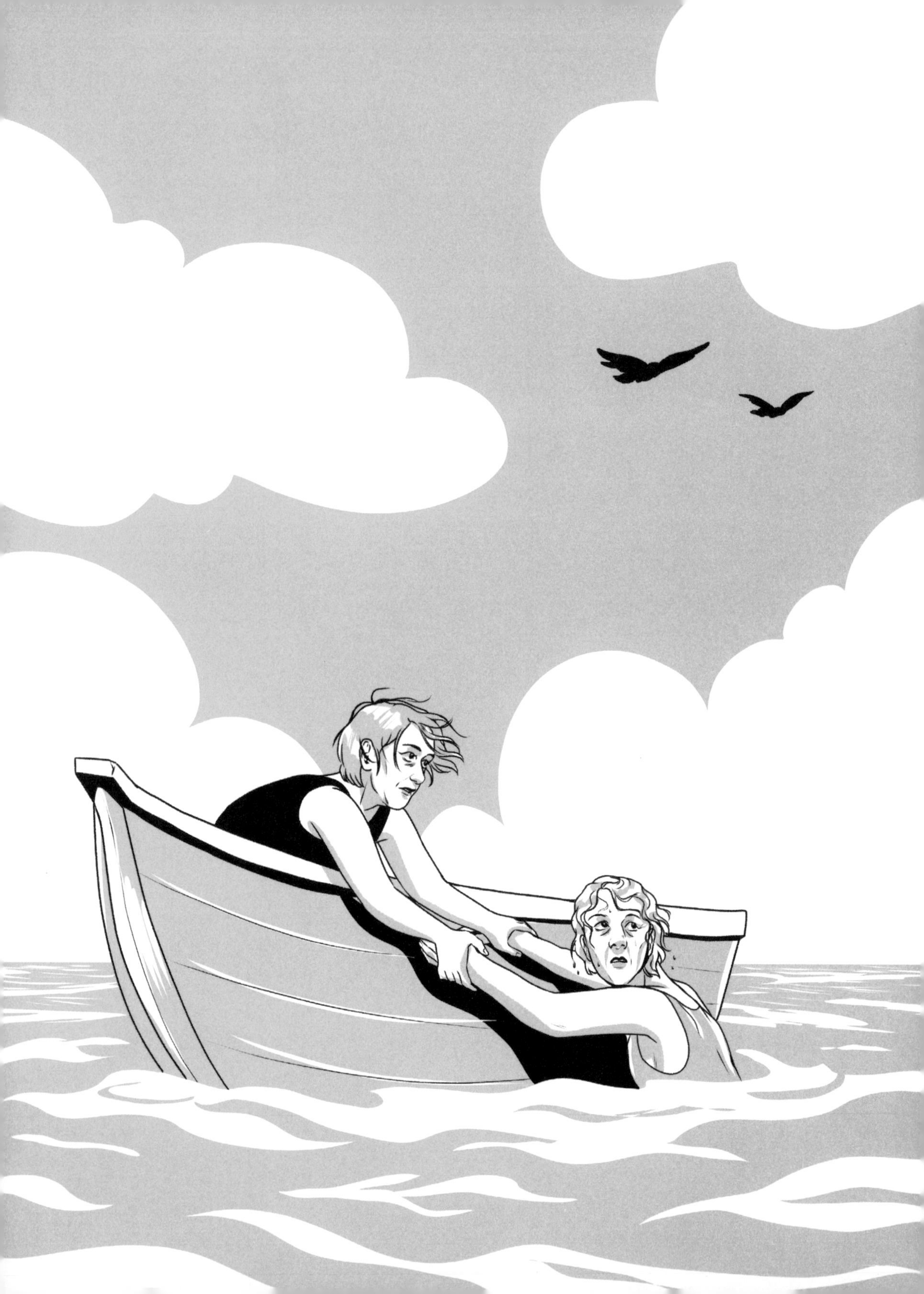

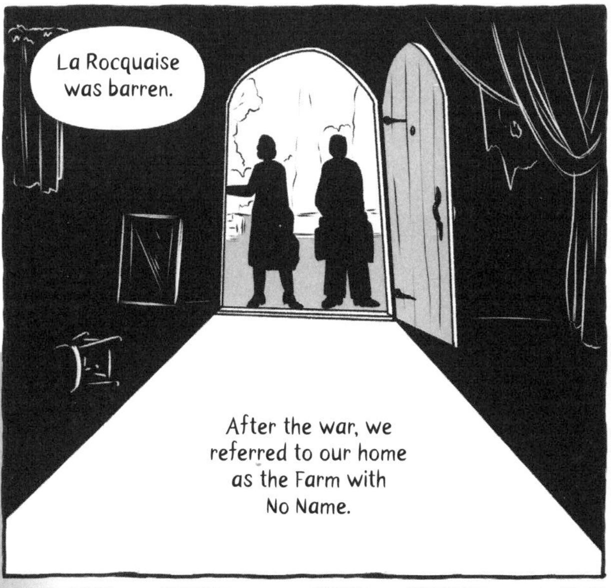
La Rocquaise was barren.
After the war, we referred to our home as the Farm with No Name.

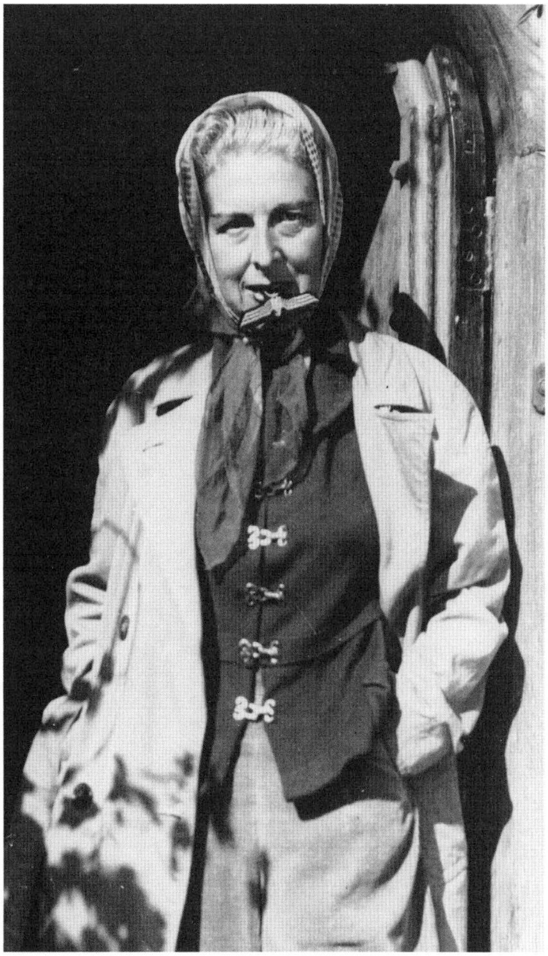

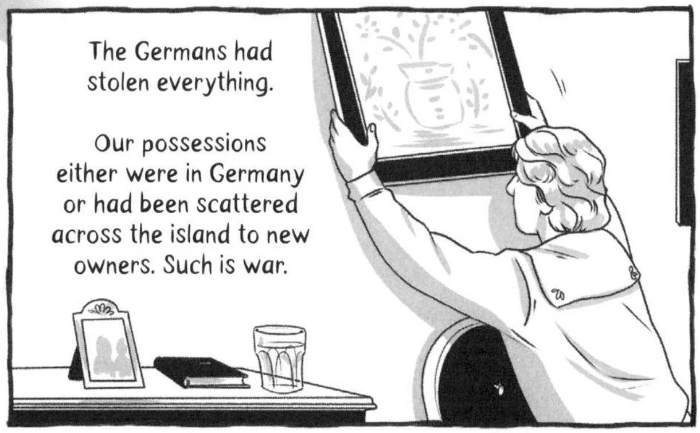
The Germans had stolen everything.
Our possessions either were in Germany or had been scattered across the island to new owners. Such is war.

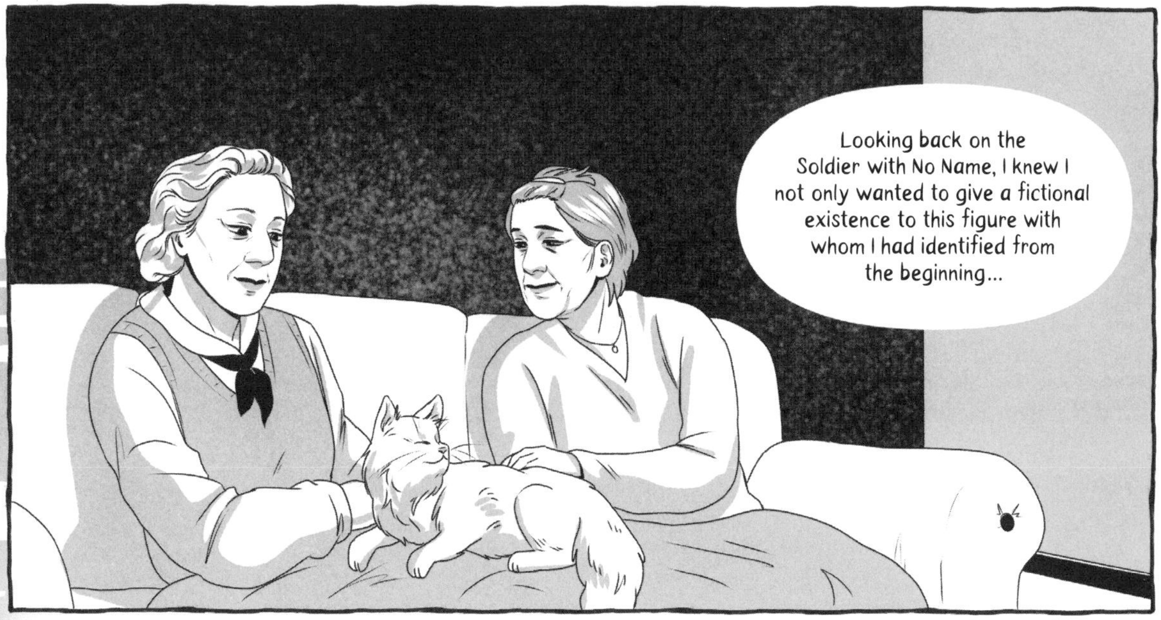
Looking back on the Soldier with No Name, I knew I not only wanted to give a fictional existence to this figure with whom I had identified from the beginning...

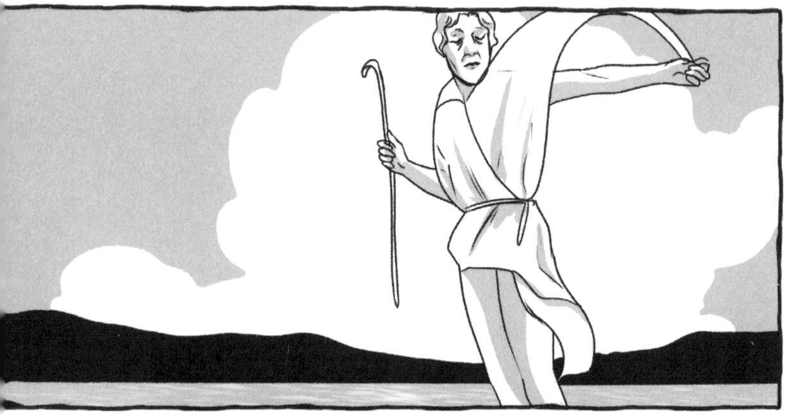

but I also wanted to furnish him a reality, breathe life into him—and in doing so suppress myself, step down in favor of him.

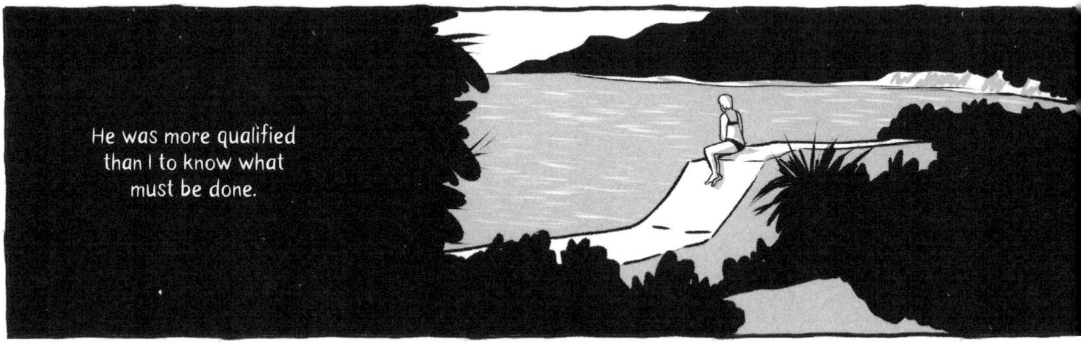
He was more qualified than I to know what must be done.

He had no name because he was everyone, every soldier, including Suzanne and me. He came from everywhere and nowhere.

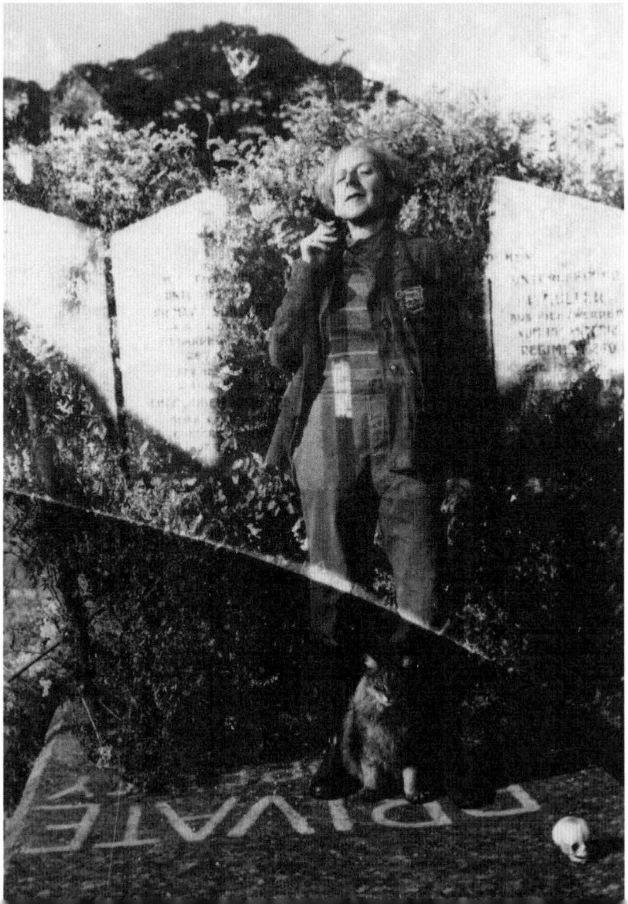

Through it all, I did my best with what I had, beginning with Surrealism and ending with Suzanne.

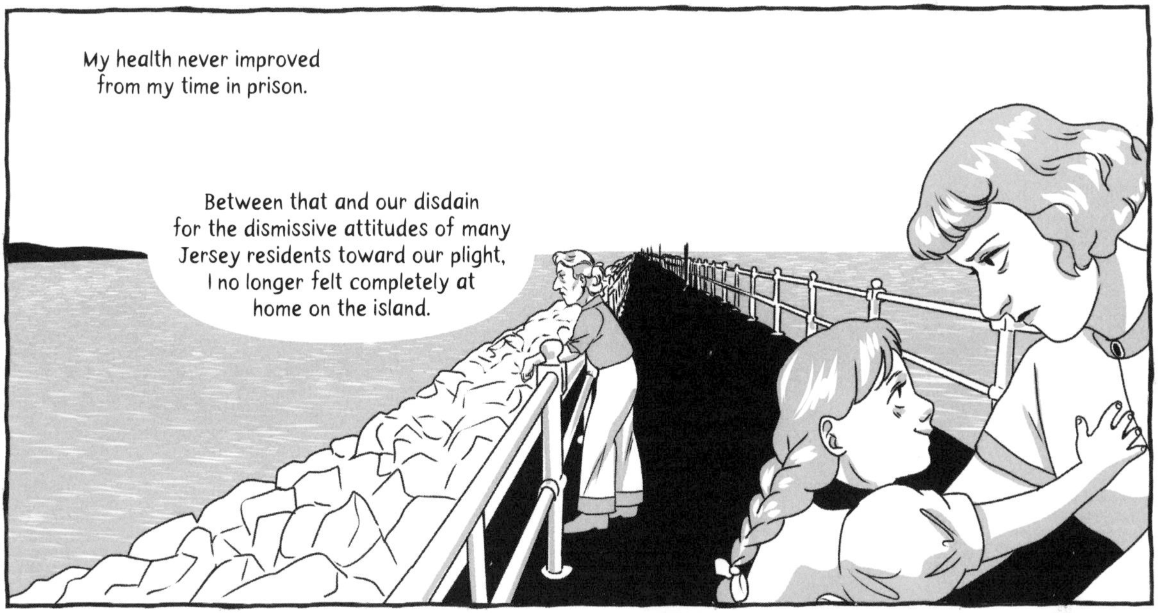
My health never improved from my time in prison.
Between that and our disdain for the dismissive attitudes of many Jersey residents toward our plight, I no longer felt completely at home on the island.

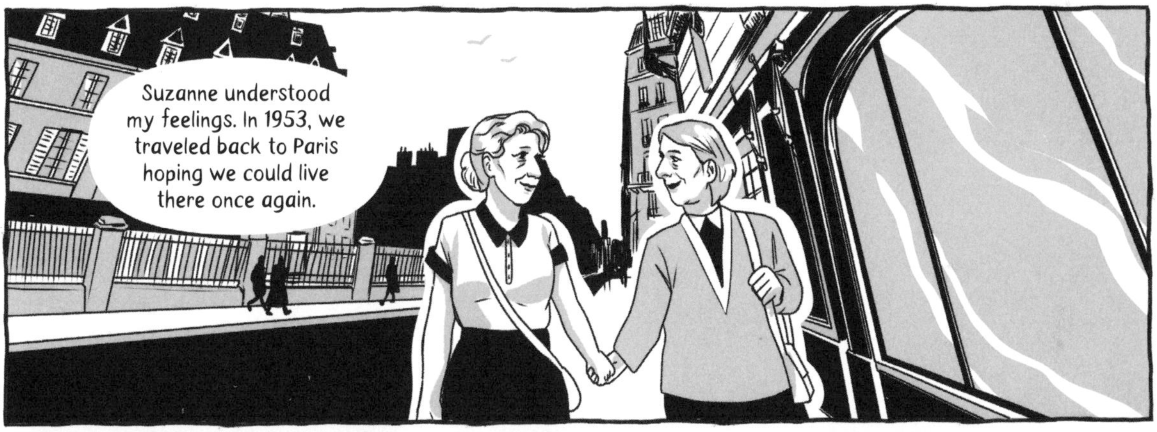
Suzanne understood my feelings. In 1953, we traveled back to Paris hoping we could live there once again.

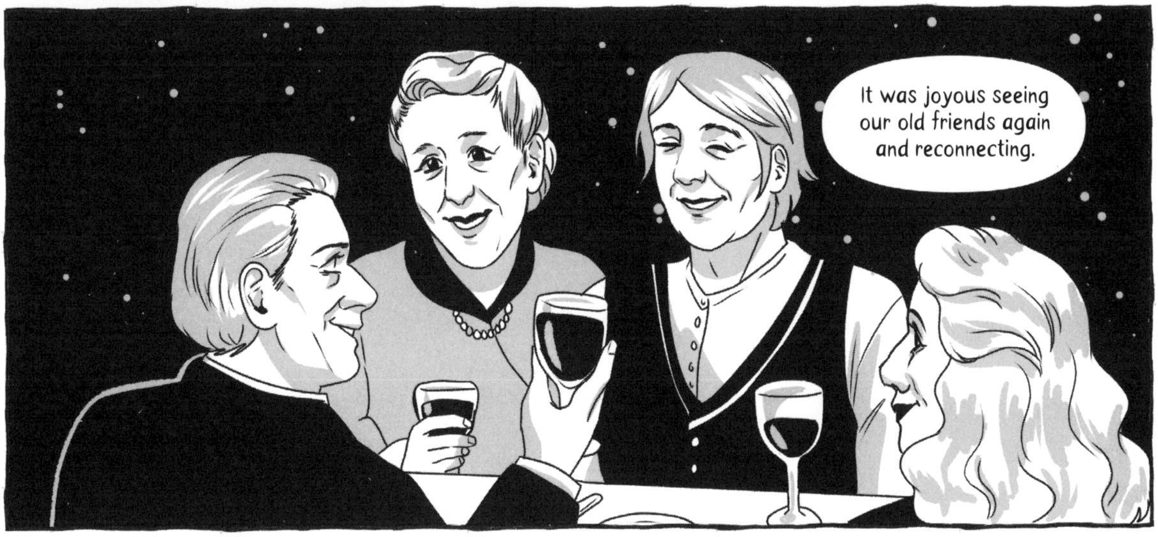
It was joyous seeing our old friends again and reconnecting.

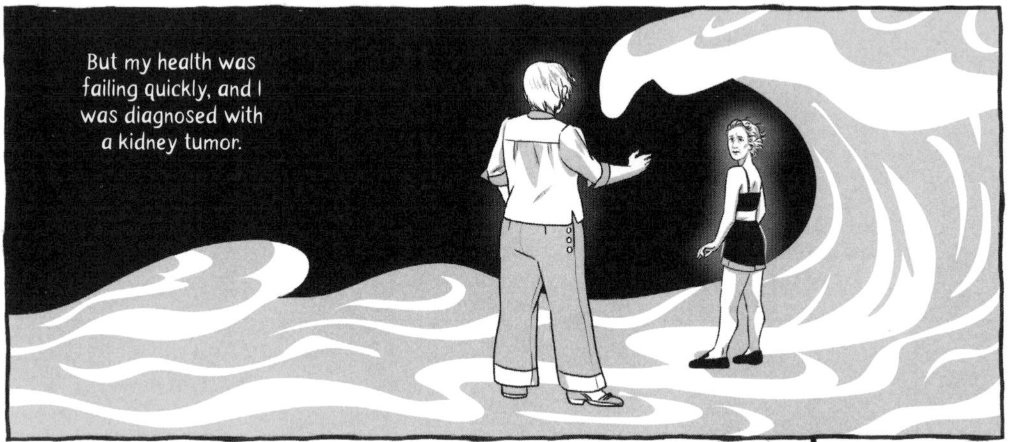
But my health was failing quickly, and I was diagnosed with a kidney tumor.

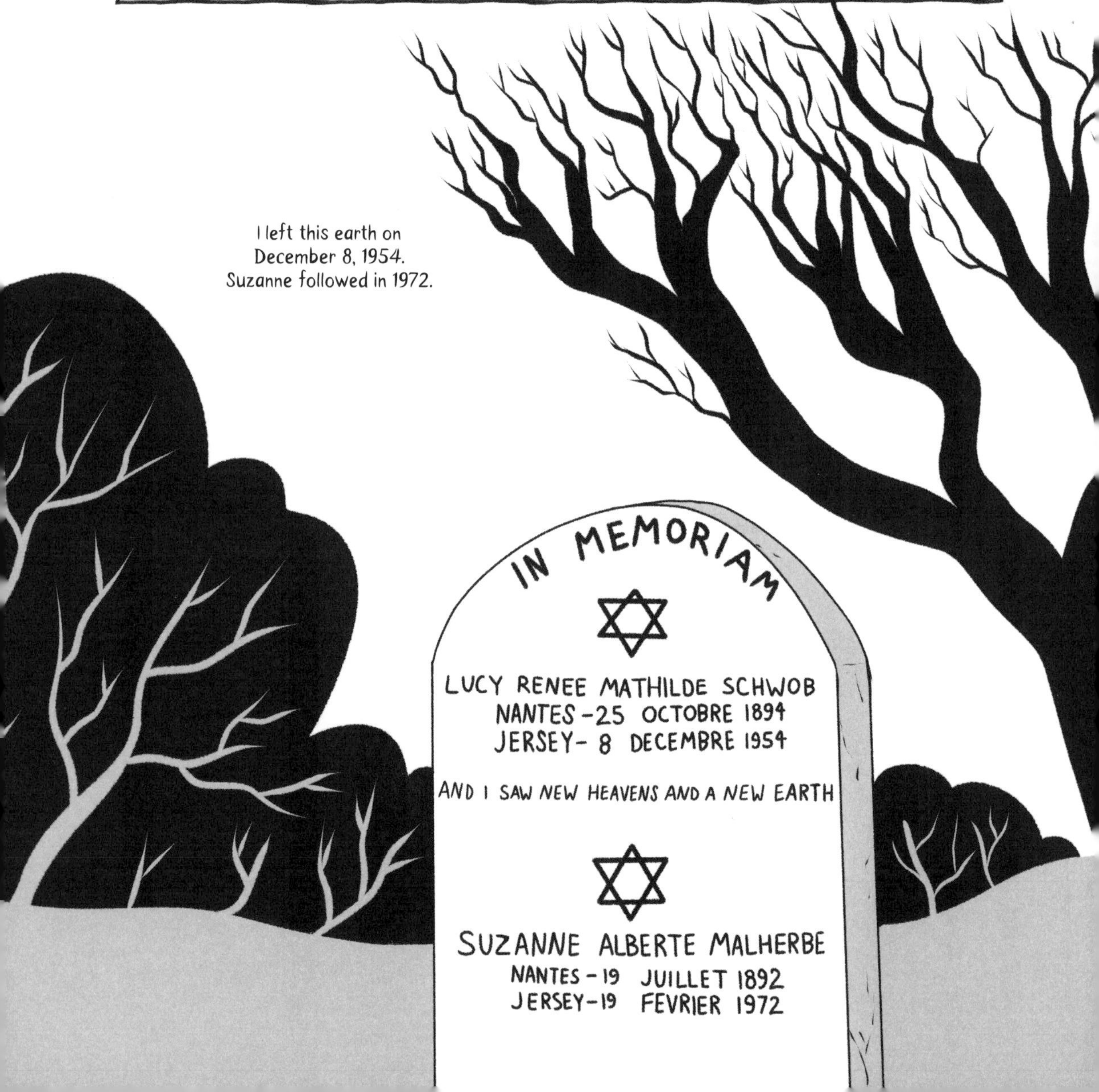
I left this earth on December 8, 1954. Suzanne followed in 1972.
IN MEMORIAM
LUCY RENEE MATHILDE SCHWOB
NANTES -25 OCTOBRE 1894
JERSEY- 8 DECEMBRE 1954
AND I SAW NEW HEAVENS AND A NEW EARTH
SUZANNE ALBERTE MALHERBE
NANTES -19 JUILLET 1892
JERSEY-19 FEVRIER 1972

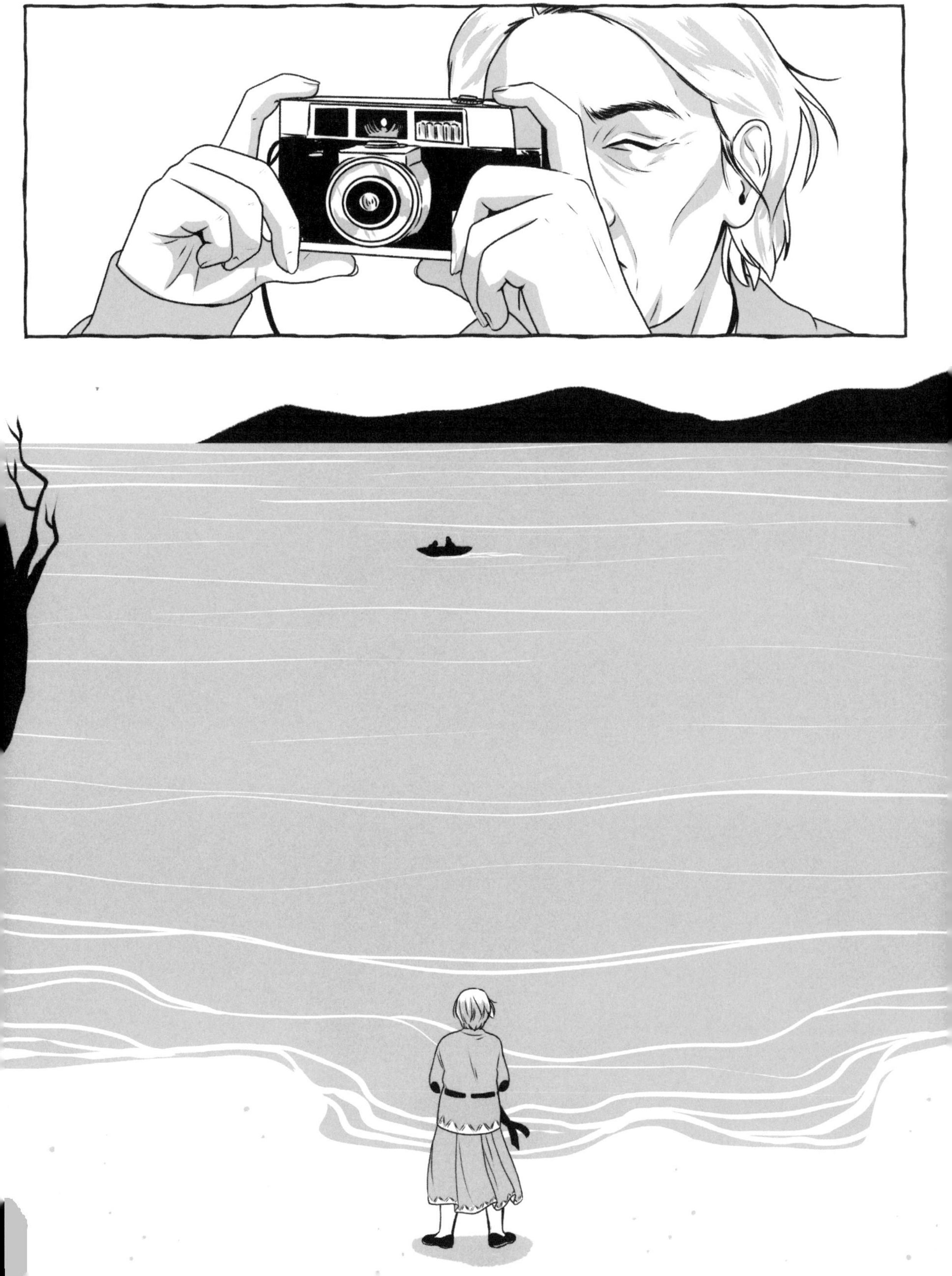

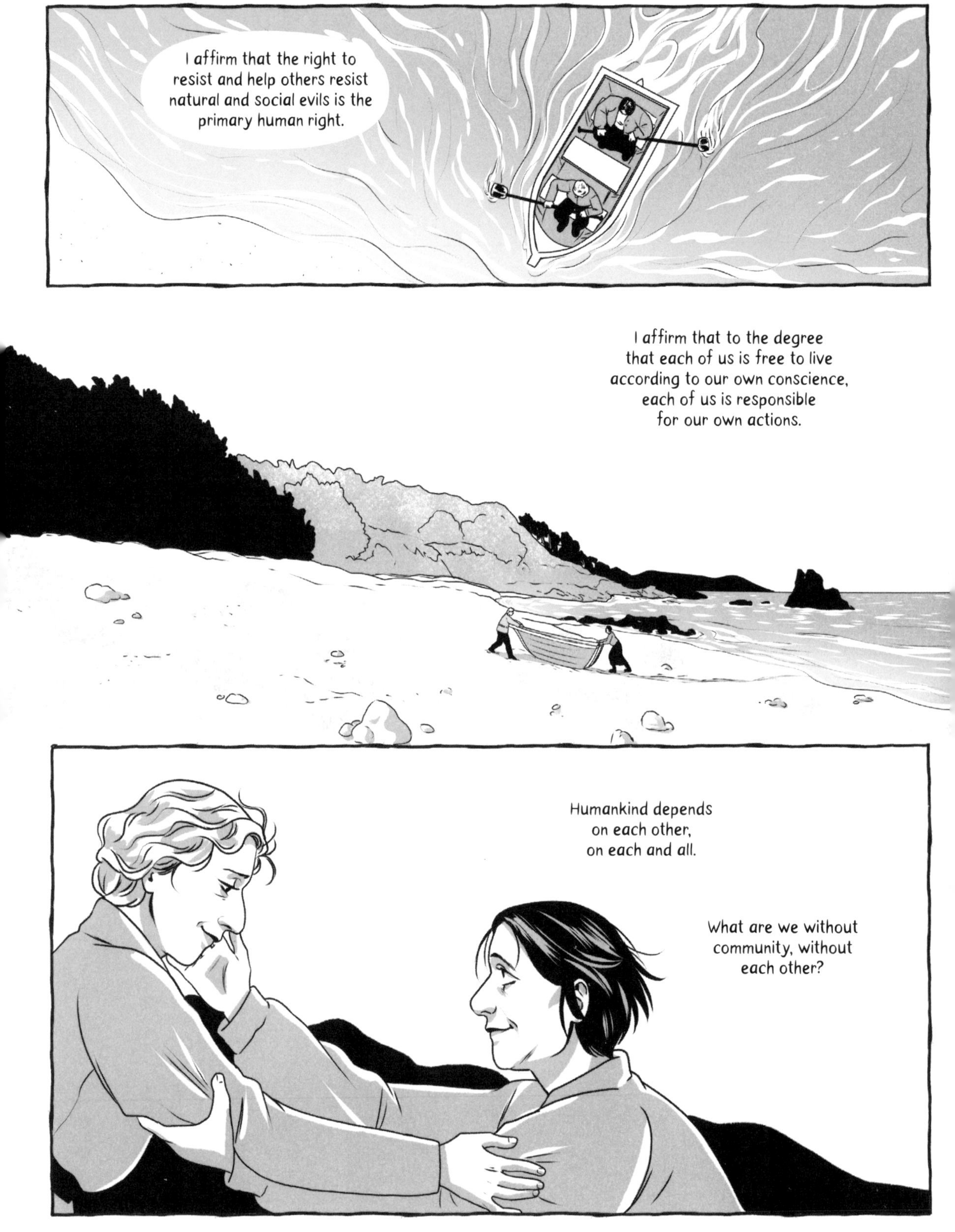
I affirm that the right to resist and help others resist natural and social evils is the primary human right.
I affirm that to the degree that each of us is free to live according to our own conscience, each of us is responsible for our own actions.
Humankind depends on each other, on each and all.
What are we without community, without each other?

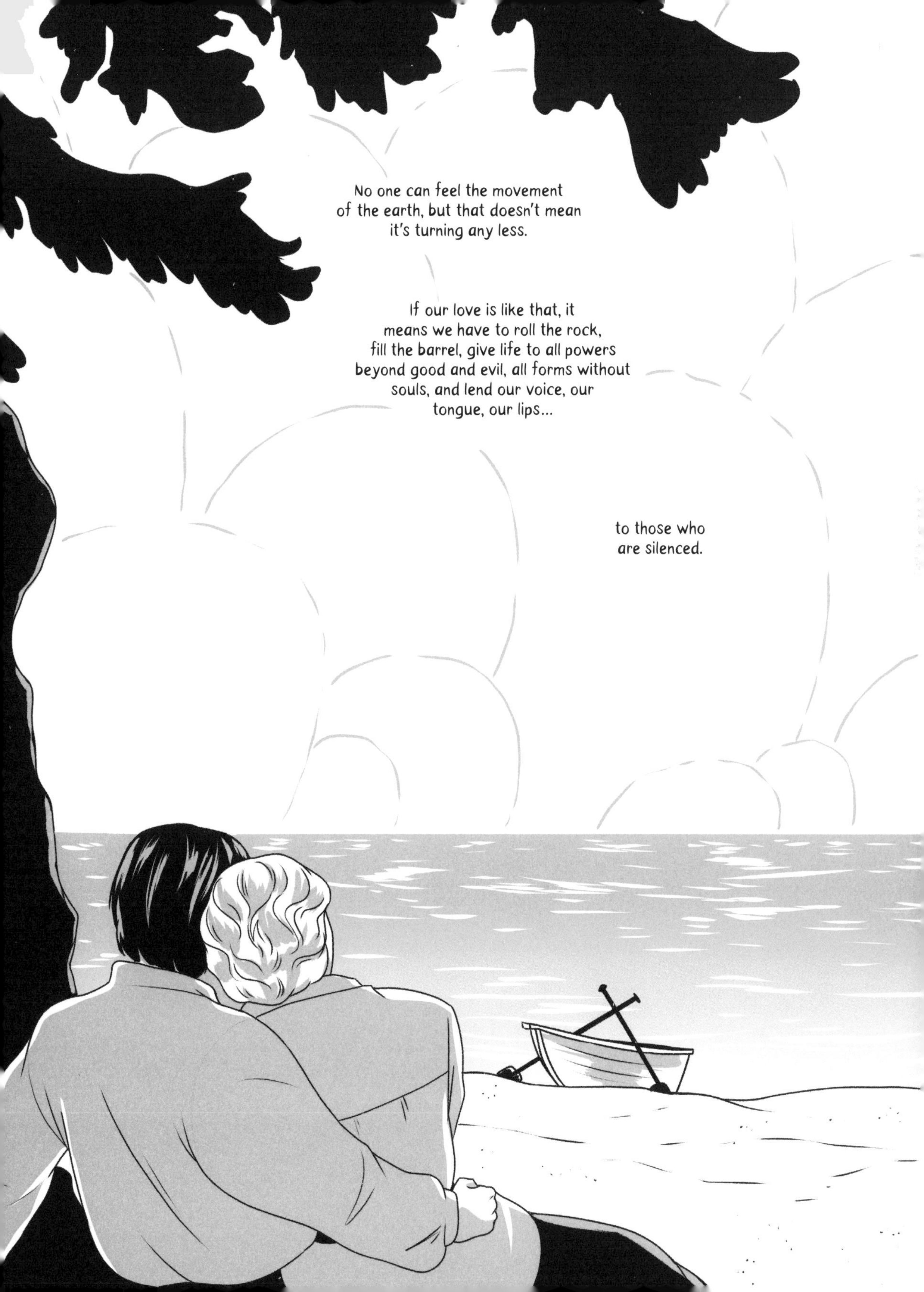
No one can feel the movement of the earth, but that doesn't mean it's turning any less.
If our love is like that, it means we have to roll the rock, fill the barrel, give life to all powers beyond good and evil, all forms without souls, and lend our voice, our tongue, our lips...
to those who are silenced.

Timeline of Key Events in the Lives of Claude Cahun and Marcel Moore

July 19, 1892	Suzanne Alberte Malherbe is born in Nantes, France, to Marie-Eugénie Rondet and Albert Hippolyte Malherbe.
1894	**The Dreyfus Affair begins with the arrest and wrongful conviction for treason of Alfred Dreyfus, a Jewish captain in the French army. The affair reflects France's deeply ingrained antisemitism and ignites a controversy that would echo through the decades to come.**
October 25, 1894	Lucy Renée Mathilde Schwob is born in Nantes, France, to Maurice Schwob and Marie-Antoinette Courbebaisse.
1897–1905	Lucy is sent to live with their grandmother Mathilde Schwob.
1906	Alfred Dreyfus's conviction is annulled, leading to antisemitic protests against Maurice Schwob's newspaper.
1908	Lucy attends to the Parsons Mead School in Surrey, England, to protect them from antisemitism in France.
Spring 1909	Lucy and Suzanne meet.
June 28, 1914	**Archduke Franz Ferdinand of Austria is assassinated in Sarajevo.**
July 28, 1914	**World War I begins.**
May 7, 1915	**British ocean liner the RMS *Lusitania* is attacked by a German U-boat and sinks.**
1915	Albert Malherbe passes away.
1917	Maurice Schwob and Marie-Eugénie Rondet marry.
1918	Lucy goes to Paris to study philosophy and letters at the Sorbonne. Suzanne studies drawing at the École des Beaux-Arts in Nantes.
November 11, 1918	**World War I ends.**
1919	Lucy and Suzanne adopt the names Claude Cahun and Marcel Moore and publish *Vues et visions* together.
1920	Cahun and Moore move to Paris and kick start their collaborative artistic career.
1925	Cahun publishes their essay series *Heroines*.
1928	Maurice Schwob passes away.
1929	**The Great Depression begins and affects Germany greatly.**
	Cahun stars in several avant-garde plays for the theater group Le Plateau.
1930	*Disavowals*, Cahun's memoir, is published in France as *Aveux non avenus*.
about 1930	Marie-Antoinette Courbebaisse passes away.
January 1932	Cahun and Moore join the Association of Revolutionary Writers and Artists (AEAR).

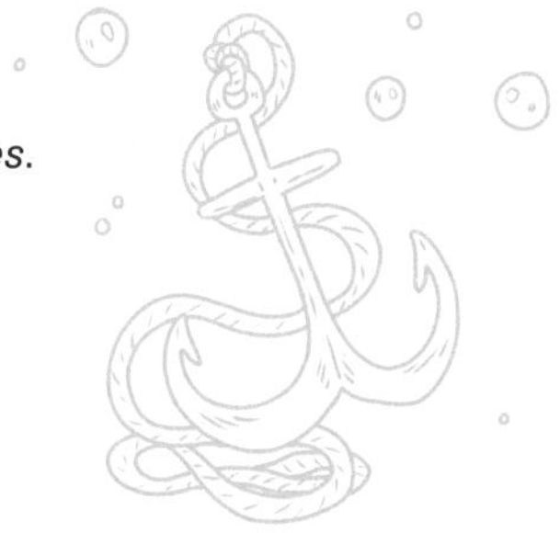

April 1932	Cahun and Moore meet André Breton, a French writer and leader of the Surrealist movement in literature and visual art.
January 30, 1933	**Adolf Hitler is appointed chancellor of Germany.**
May 25, 1934	Cahun publishes *Les Paris sont ouverts* (Bets are Open), a discussion of politics and literature.
October 7, 1935	Cahun and Moore, among others, form Contre-Attaque, a group of Surrealists, dissidents, and intellectuals united against fascism.
1936	Marie-Eugénie Rondet passes away.
Summer 1936–37	Cahun works with Lise Deharme to create illustrations for *Le Coeur de pic*.
March 1937	Cahun and Moore move to Jersey, an English island off the coast of France.
March 1938	**Germany annexes Austria.**
May 1938	Cahun joins the International Federation of Independent Revolutionary Art.
September 1, 1939	**Hitler invades Poland. World War II begins.**
May 1940	**The Nazis invade and occupy France.**
June 30, 1940	**The Nazis begin occupation of Jersey.**
December 7, 1941	**The Imperial Japanese Army bombs Pearl Harbor. The United States joins the war.**
1942	Cahun and Moore begin their secret resistance activities under Nazi occupation.
March 1944	Cahun is ordered to report to the Kommandantur, the Nazi headquarters in Jersey.
June 6, 1944	**D-Day. The Allied forces land on the coast of Normandy, France.**
July 25, 1944	Cahun and Moore are arrested by the Gestapo and sent to prison.
November 16, 1944	Cahun and Moore's trial concludes, and they are sentenced to death.
May 8, 1945	**Liberation Day, also known as Victory in Europe Day (V-E Day). The Allied forces accept Germany's surrender.**
	Cahun and Moore are freed from prison.
September 2, 1945	**World War II ends with Japan's surrender.**
1953	Cahun and Moore visit Paris again.
December 8, 1954	Claude Cahun passes away.
February 19, 1972	Marcel Moore passes away.

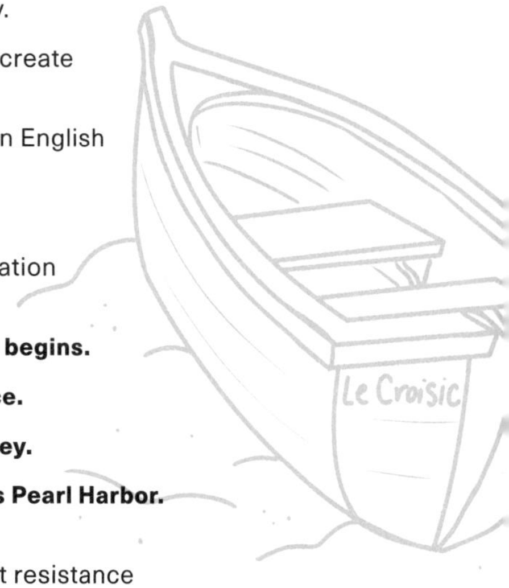
Le Croisic

Note from the Author on Sources

In taking on Claude Cahun's incredible story, I wanted to make sure that Cahun's voice remained prominent. Cahun and Marcel Moore left behind a wealth of direct writings—diaries, letters, memoirs, manifestos, and notes, some that managed to survive World War II and some that were written after Liberation to make up for what was lost. Direct quotes from both Cahun and Moore are interwoven into the narration and dialogue throughout and are not singled out so as not to distract from the story, as this is first and foremost a work of creative graphic nonfiction. However, if you would like to read more of Cahun's and Moore's own words, they can be found in the sources listed in the bibliography. I heartily encourage you to do so, as there are so many amazing details about their lives that I was unable to include here.

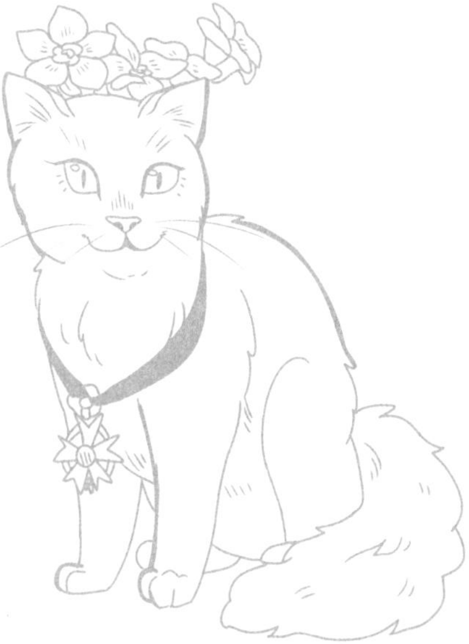

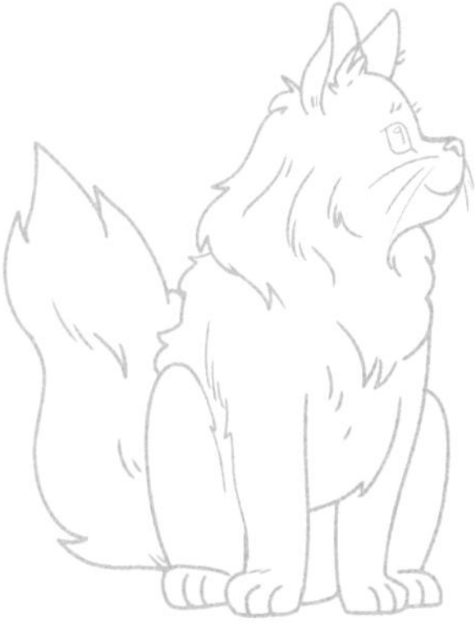

Bibliography

Cahun, Claude, et al. *Claude Cahun Aveux non avenus: Illustré d'hélio-gravures composées par Moore d'après les projets de l'auteur.* Paris: Éditions du Carrefour, 1930.

Cahun, Claude. *Disavowals, or Cancelled Confessions.* Edited by Jennifer Mundy. Translated by Susan de Muth. Cambridge, MA: MIT Press, 2008.

Chadwick, Whitney. *The Militant Muse: Love, War and the Women of Surrealism.* London: Thames & Hudson, 2021.

Conley, Katharine. "Claude Cahun's Exploration of the Autobiographical Human." In *Surrealist Ghostliness*, 45–68. Lincoln: University of Nebraska Press, 2013.

Dean, Carolyn J. "Claude Cahun's Double." *Yale French Studies*, no. 90 (1996): 71–92.

Jackson, Jeffrey H. *Paper Bullets: Two Artists Who Risked Their Lives to Defy the Nazis.* Chapel Hill, NC: Algonquin Books, 2021.

Knafo, Danielle. "Claude Cahun: The Third Sex." *Studies in Gender and Sexuality* 2, no. 1 (2001): 29–61.

Latimer, Tirza True. *Women Together/Women Apart: Portraits of Lesbian Paris.* New Brunswick, NJ: Rutgers University Press, 2005.

Rice, Shelley, ed. *Inverted Odysseys: Claude Cahun, Maya Deren, and Cindy Sherman.* Cambridge, MA: MIT Press, 1999.

Shaw, Jennifer Laurie. *Exist Otherwise: The Life and Works of Claude Cahun.* London: Reaktion Books, 2017.

Wampole, Christy. "The Impudence of Claude Cahun." *L'Esprit créateur* 53, no. 1 (2013): 101–13.

Welby-Everard, Miranda. "Imaging the Actor: The Theatre of Claude Cahun." *Oxford Art Journal* 29, no. 1 (2006): 3–24.

Author Bio

Kaz Rowe is a cartoonist, an illustrator, and a YouTuber. Kaz grew up in Coppell, Texas, and Los Angeles and earned their BFA from the School of the Art Institute of Chicago (SAIC) with a focus on film production, writing, painting, and comics. At SAIC, Kaz rediscovered their love of history and research, completing their degree in 2018 with a mini-comic biography of the gay illustrator J. C. Leyendecker, *He Lives in the Echoes*. Kaz has also produced a long-form urban fantasy webcomic called *Cunning Fire* since 2016 and was a contributor to *Group Chat: A Comics Anthology about Friendship and Found Family* (POME Press, 2018). Kaz became a YouTuber during the production of *Liberated* and enjoys making educational videos about strange, underrepresented, and queer histories. Their love of storytelling, comics, and history has made it a great privilege to adapt the incredible life of Claude Cahun into visual form.

@kazrowe on Twitter | @kaz.rowe on Instagram | Kaz Rowe on YouTube

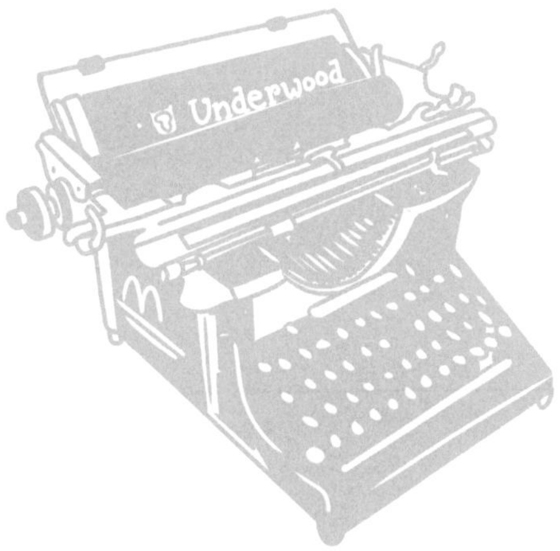
Underwood

Acknowledgments

Kaz would like to thank Getty for asking them to helm this fantastic project about a historical figure so close to their heart. Thank you to Ruth Evans Lane for being such an incredibly supportive editor and guide in making this project possible, and to Tirza True Latimer and Audrey Warne for providing much-needed research support in the early stages. Thank you to Jim Drobka, Amy McFarland, Molly McGeehan, Leslie Rollins, Maureen Winter, Sydney Almaraz-Neal, Dina Murokh, Karen Levine, and everyone else at Getty Publications who helped bring this book to life. And thank you to the Jersey Heritage Trust for entrusting us with everything we needed to make this project happen.

Kaz would also like to thank their parents, Leslie and Brandon Rowe, as well as their grandma Gail Gegna, for all their support during the making of this graphic biography and long, long before it. They are also lovingly grateful to their grandpa Mike Gegna, whose life story as a Holocaust survivor made it ever more meaningful to take on Cahun's biography. Though he will not be able to read it, his presence is on every page.

Lastly, thank you to Claude Cahun and Marcel Moore for leaving us this breathtaking life story to share. Their impact is felt and it is lasting, and their bravery continues to be an inspiration.

List of Photographs

Many of the illustrations in this book are drawn from and inspired by the works of Claude Cahun and Marcel Moore. All photographs are by Claude Cahun and Marcel Moore and courtesy of and © the Jersey Heritage Collections. unless otherwise noted.

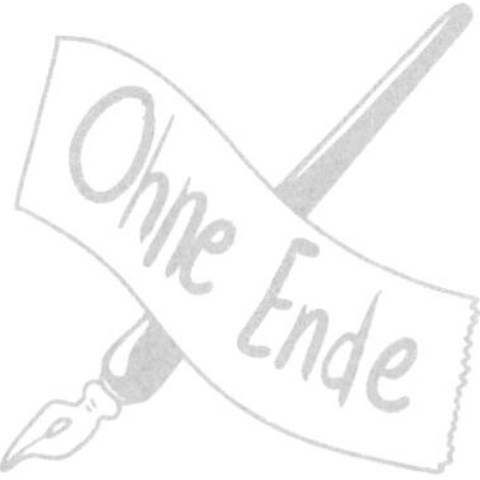
Ohne Ende

Published by Getty Publications, Los Angeles
1200 Getty Center Drive, Suite 500
Los Angeles, California 90049-1682
getty.edu/publications

Ruth Evans Lane, *Editor*
Jim Drobka and Amy McFarland, *Designers*
Molly McGeehan, *Production*
Leslie Rollins, *Image and Rights Acquisition*

Distributed in North America by ABRAMS, New York
Distributed outside North America by Yale University Press, London

Printed in Italy

Library of Congress Cataloging-in-Publication Data
Names: Rowe, Kaz, 1996– author.
Title: Liberated : the radical art and life of Claude Cahun / Kaz Rowe.
Description: Los Angeles : Getty Publications, [2023] | Includes bibliographical references. | Audience: Ages 12 and up. | Audience: Grades 10–12. | Summary: "This graphic biography chronicles the life of Surrealist artist Claude Cahun, from their childhood and experiences of antisemitism in France, through the development of their artistic practice in Paris, to their resistance against the Nazis in Jersey, and includes photographs by Cahun and artistic and romantic partner Marcel Moore"— Provided by publisher.
Identifiers: LCCN 2022039450 (print) | LCCN 2022039451 (ebook) | ISBN 9781947440074 (hardcover) | ISBN 9781606068533 (adobe pdf) | ISBN 9781606068540 (epub)
Subjects: LCSH: Cahun, Claude, 1894–1954—Comic books, strips, etc. | Moore, Marcel, 1892–1972—Comic books, strips, etc. | Artists—France—Biography—Comic books, strips, etc. | Lesbian artists—France—Biography—Comic books, strips, etc. | Artist couples—France—Biography—Comic books, strips, etc. | Gender-nonconforming people—France—Biography—Comic books, strips, etc. | World War, 1939–1945—Underground movements—Jersey—Comic books, strips, etc. | Channel Islands—History—German occupation, 1940–1945—Comic books, strips, etc. | LCGFT: Biographical comics. | Graphic novels.
Classification: LCC N6853.C252 R69 2023 (print) | LCC N6853.C252 (ebook) | DDC 709.2 [B]—dc23/eng/20221018
LC record available at https://lccn.loc.gov/2022039450
LC ebook record available at https://lccn.loc.gov/2022039451